Living
the
SPIRIT
FILLED
LIFE®

Living
the
SPIRIT
FILLED
LIFE®

JACK W. HAYFORD

THOMAS NELSON PUBLISHERS
Nashville

Published in Nashville, Tennessee, by Thomas Nelson, Inc.

Unless otherwise indicated, all Scripture quotations are from the *New King James Version*, copyright © 1979, 1980, 1982, 1990 by Thomas Nelson, Inc.

Book design and composition by Bob Bubnis, Booksetters, White House, Tennessee

Hayford, Jack W.

   Living the Spirit-filled Life

ISBN: 0-7852-4938-9

Printed in the United States of America

1 2 3 4 5 6 7 — 06 05 04 03 02

INTRODUCTION:
Knowing the Beauty of the Lord Our God

You want a Bible study that does more than teach you Bible history and theological facts. You want a study that leads into a breathtaking encounter with God. Don't you? Who doesn't? You want to end up with more than another book on your shelf with the answer blanks filled in. You want to open rooms in your heart and turn on lights in your soul that will enlarge your spiritual life. Don't you? Who doesn't? You want more than platitudes about power and liberty. You want some keys to the locks that bind your spirit so you can be free. Don't you? Who doesn't?

The written Word of God tells us about God on paper. Jesus, the living Word of God, put skin on God and showed Him to us. The Bible and the Holy Spirit point us to Jesus for the simple reason that Jesus makes God's character and heart plain to us. Our complaints *Why did God let this happen?* never find any good answers until we ask *Who was Jesus and how did He respond to this kind of pain?* Our longings for lasting peace and abiding satisfaction will never be met through a seminar at the Hilton or by a call to a psychic hotline. Those longings are satisfied in Jesus. This workbook will point you toward intimacy with Jesus, your Savior from sin and your Lord of life.

As you become intimate with Jesus, He will point you beyond Himself to His Father. While He lived on earth, Jesus showed us the Father by doing the Father's will. Jesus taught us to pray, *Our Father in heaven, . . . Your will be done on earth as it is in heaven* (Matt. 6:9, 10). If you wonder why you don't feel close to the Father—even when you feel close to Jesus—it may be that you haven't grasped the importance of doing the will of God. Your heart will only beat with the Father's when the goal of your one and only life is to do His will *on earth as it is in heaven*. The kingdom of God encompasses your life when you do the Father's will. This workbook will guide your exploration into the will of God for your friendships, your family life, your career, and your ministry.

Jesus carried out the will of His Father in the power of the Holy Spirit (Luke 3:22; 4:1, 14, 18; 10:21). The twentieth century witnessed a revival of Spirit-empowered living and ministry among Christian laypeople and clergy that cut across denominational lines and leaped oceans and mountain ranges to span the globe. As the twenty-first century opens, the Spirit of God longs to continue lifting up the Son and energizing believers to find their place in the Father's will and experience the reign of God in their lives. This workbook will help you encounter the Spirit as the filler, anointer, and energizer of God's people.

Deeper and Higher

At the end of *The Last Battle*, Aslan the Lion leads his followers—children, animals, and creatures—through a magic door into a strange land that seems oddly familiar. As Aslan bounds away, he roars over his shoulder, "Come further in! Come further up!" They all hurry after Aslan, but he is soon lost to sight. They continue on an uphill course.

"Don't stop! Further up and further in!" Farsight, the eagle calls out, urging the children and creatures up the mountainside toward Aslan's land. From his vantage point overhead and with his sharp eyes, he sees magnificent vistas ahead.

"Don't stop! Further up and further in! Take it in your stride," cries one of the children as a sheer cliff blocks their path. A waterfall plunges from the dizzying height into a pool. All leap into the crystal depths to find they can swim up the waterfall to the high country.

"Further up and further in!" trumpets a unicorn as he leads them in a final charge across mountain valleys and streams to the golden gates of Aslan's city.

"Welcome in the Lion's name. Come further up and further in," says Reepicheep the heroic mouse as he invites them into the very presence of Aslan.

One of C. S. Lewis' great accomplishments was challenging his readers to realize what an adventure pursuing a relationship with God is. Aslan is a lion, and it is never entirely safe to be around a lion. But Aslan is good. His great power can be trusted but never trifled with or—worse yet—ignored. The Spirit-filled Christian life is such an adventure, because it opens itself to receive the power of God and share it with others.

The Christian life can be summarized as giving all that I know of myself to all that I know of God. When you accepted Jesus as your Savior, you probably knew more about yourself than you did about Him. It's likely that you also had some wrong ideas on what you were like. Maybe you had some goofy ideas about God, too.

How about now? In the time since your salvation experience, have you grown in your self-awareness? Have you continued to surrender all of yourself to the Lord? This workbook will hold up the mirror of God's Word to give you opportunity to see your heart and your soul more clearly (Heb. 4:12; James 1:23–25). Whatever you discover about yourself—warts and all—give it to the Lord.

Sure you know more about God than when you first came to saving faith. But has your knowledge curve kept up with the needs of your life? How often life's next big jolt finds us deficient in faith, hope, or love and we let go of God's Hand as the bottom drops out. He doesn't let go of us, but we can feel alone as we struggle to deal with our crisis. This workbook is designed to be proactive. Let it help you grow up in your knowledge of Father, Son, and Spirit so you have much more of Him to give yourself to. You'll be better prepared for life's next big bump.

Let this workbook guide you in listening to the still small voice of God's Spirit. We live in a noisy, hectic culture that wants us to conform to its tightly planned, multi-tasking, immediate gratification mindset. The Bible calls us to be quiet before God, wait for His time and place, worship at His feet, meditate on His Word, and sense His voice in the silence. Elijah had to tune out a cyclone, an earthquake, and a firestorm before he heard God whisper (1 Kin. 19:11, 12).

Let the Word of God and the Spirit of God call you further up and further in as you use *Living the Spirit-Filled Life*® as a discipleship tool. The psalmist prayed, *And let the beauty of the LORD our God be upon us, and establish the work of our hands for us; yes, establish the work of our hands* (Ps. 90:17). What lasts, what is established forever, comes from *the beauty of the LORD our God*. We find that transforming beauty as we go further up and further into the Word of God in response to the Spirit of God.

A Planned Encounter

Living the Spirit-Filled Life® is a resource, and you will get from these spiritual exercises what you put into them. Here are some pointers for maximizing your investment.

This workbook is designed for individual rather than group study. You need to allow enough time for each day's activity to permit meditation on the Scripture and on your responses to God's Word and Spirit.

Each chapter of *Living the Spirit-Filled Life®* provides spiritual exercises for one week, so the whole study occupies eight weeks. Each chapter contains five daily studies. Every study develops an aspect of the theme for the week. You might want to study Monday through Friday and use the two weekend days for additional meditation. Choose a time of day and a place of study that can be fairly consistent and allow yourself time to be quiet before God. You may wish to consider using *The New Spirit-Filled Life® Bible* along with this workbook. Its many features will greatly enhance the value of the exercises found in this volume.

Within the daily studies, you will encounter four basic components. You will study various passages of Scripture pertaining to the day's topic. These provide the raw materials from the heart of God for you to respond to. Then you will follow prayer and meditation activities to help you listen to the Word of God. Next you will journal your responses to the Word and your meditation in the spaces provided in your workbook. You may want to use a notebook as a companion to *Living the Spirit-Filled Life®* so you have more room to record your thoughts. Finally, you will formulate action plans for implementing what you learn in your daily life and in your ministry at your church or in other outreach opportunities. These four components interweave, so don't expect four distinct sections to each study.

Living the Spirit-Filled Life® can guide you through the internal phases of the cycle of spiritual growth. The behavioral aspects of growth—obedience to Word and Spirit—will happen after you close your Bible and your workbook and put them on your bookshelf. The real growth happens when you talk to your family, spend your money, do your job, help your neighbors, and share your faith. Maybe people will sense the beauty of the Lord your God upon you.

Memos

Scattered through *Living the Spirit-Filled Life*® are features called *Memos* to encourage you and stimulate your spirit. They're like the sticky notes many people tack all over their work stations, dashboards, mirrors, or refrigerators to remind themselves of jobs and ideas. Probably not all of the Memos in this workbook will be equally relevant to you. Appreciate the ones that resonate with you and hope the others are helpful to others.

Listen to the Spirit contains brief devotional thoughts to tune your spirit to the topic for the day.

Heart Sounds challenge you to consider the emotional impact of the truth you are evaluating.

Grace Notes tell stories of God's Word and Spirit at work in others.

Insight provide historical background, explain difficult theological terms, or give other information necessary to deal with Scripture in the workbook.

A New Song expresses praise or contains prayers directed to God in response to the subject being studied.

Godspeed

The languages of western civilization have greetings and farewells acknowledging the Christian heritage of their speakers. Spanish speakers say *Vaya con Dios* and *Adios*. The French say *Adieu*. Bavarians and Austrians say *Grüss Gott*. We English speakers used to say *Godspeed*. *Godspeed* is a short form of the sentence "God speed you on your journey." It's not a wish for haste—that's a modern obsession. It's a prayer for safety and blessing.

May you have *Godspeed* as you journey through *Living the Spirit-Filled Life*®. May God bless you and bring you safely further up and further in.

SPIRIT-FILLED HOLINESS

We call Him the *Holy* Spirit of God. So if we're going to lead a Spirit-filled life, we probably need to take seriously the business of being holy. What makes the Spirit holy? What is holiness? How do we get it? What does it look like, feel like, act like? Do we really want to be holy, or will holiness make us weird?

In the introduction to this workbook, we used the expression "further up and further in" from *The Chronicles of Narnia* to express the spiritual longing that reaches both toward God and into the human heart to unite the two in unspeakable peace and joy. Holiness is completely "natural" to humanity, as God created us. Any unnatural feel to holiness comes from how cozy we have become with the "alien" (by design) state of spiritual corruption.

The power of God's holiness transforms us as we embrace it and incorporate holiness into our daily living. Are you ready to be changed?

A New Song

WHO MAY ASCEND INTO THE HILL OF THE LORD? OR WHO MAY STAND IN HIS HOLY PLACE? HE WHO HAS CLEAN HANDS AND A PURE HEART, WHO HAS NOT LIFTED UP HIS SOUL TO AN IDOL, NOR SWORN DECEITFULLY. HE SHALL RECEIVE BLESSING FROM THE LORD, AND RIGHTEOUSNESS FROM THE GOD OF HIS SALVATION. THIS IS JACOB, THE GENERATION OF THOSE WHO SEEK HIM, WHO SEEK YOUR FACE.

—*Psalm 24:3–6*

THE HOLINESS OF GOD

IN THE PHYSICAL world there are certain irreducible properties that cannot be analyzed or explained. They just are. Space, time, and gravity are irreducibly fundamental physical properties. In the realm of psychology, human self-consciousness seems to be an irreducible property. Consciousness is more than brain chemistry and electro-neurological impulses. Consciousness uses these things but transcends them. In the realm of theology, holiness is an irreducibly fundamental characteristic of God. We start here in reflecting on the Spirit-filled life, because holiness is spiritual bedrock.

God marks His possessions with a seal of ownership. That seal is the Holy Spirit who takes up residence in every child of God. We are made holy by the transforming presence of the Spirit.

Because we are people, not inanimate possessions, we also take on the character of God as we associate with Him. Holiness is a family trait that eager children learn from their Father as they try to be like Him.

Let's embark on a week's exploration of the signature quality of the Spirit-filled life—holiness.

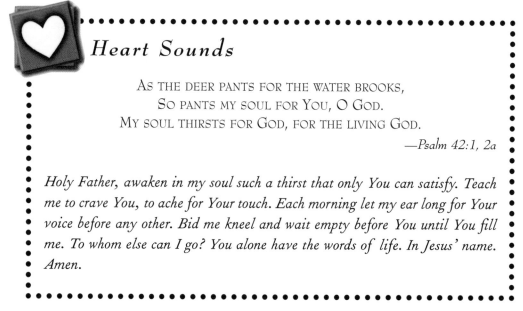

Heart Sounds

> AS THE DEER PANTS FOR THE WATER BROOKS,
> SO PANTS MY SOUL FOR YOU, O GOD.
> MY SOUL THIRSTS FOR GOD, FOR THE LIVING GOD.
>
> —*Psalm 42:1, 2a*

Holy Father, awaken in my soul such a thirst that only You can satisfy. Teach me to crave You, to ache for Your touch. Each morning let my ear long for Your voice before any other. Bid me kneel and wait empty before You until You fill me. To whom else can I go? You alone have the words of life. In Jesus' name. Amen.

1. The Bible portrays God's holiness in terms of majesty and splendor. Read the three primary biblical visions of God and His holiness. Jot down what each person saw. Note the similarities and differences between the visions.

Isaiah 6:1–4

Ezekiel 1:22–28

Revelation 4:2–11

2. Spend some time talking with God and pondering why God should reveal Himself and His holiness in terms of dazzling light broken into the colors of the spectrum, an exalted throne, thunder and lightening, a shape suggesting a human figure, and the object of worship by heavenly beings. At the end of that time, record your thoughts.

Dazzling light

An exalted throne

Thunder and lightening

A figure like a human

An object of worship

3.   How did each of these biblical figures who saw a vision of God's holiness respond to it?

Isaiah (Is. 6:5–8)

Ezekiel (Ezek. 1:28—2:1; 2:9—3:3, 14, 15)

John (Rev. 1:17–19)

4. On the following scale of 1 to 10, how would you rate your normal, daily awareness of God's dazzling holiness?

1	2	3	4	5	6	7	8	9	10
Blackout		Glimpses		Dim Bulb		Dawning Light			Bright Day

5. Circle the devotional disciplines on this list that help you focus on the holiness of God. If other activities aid you in adoration, add them to your list.

Listening to Christian music

Reading the Psalms

Fasting

Contemplating Christian art

Reading devotional classics

Viewing Christian drama or videos

Burning candles or incense during devotional activities

Kneeling or lying prostrate

6. Look at the items you circled in the previous exercise. Put a star beside the one(s) you sense God would have you employ during the rest of this week as you focus on His holiness. Take a moment to write down how you will implement your starred discipline(s) tomorrow.

Insight

The English word *holy* translates the Hebrew adjective *qadosh* and the Greek adjective *agios*. Both original words indicate that which is sacred because it belongs to God in contrast to what belongs to the world or the devil. God is *holy*; He sets the standard for distinction from the ordinary. People become *holy* when God redeems them from sin and claims them as His. The ethical, moral, and righteous connotations of *holy* arise because God cannot abide pride, falsehood, and rebellion—the hallmarks of Satan and the world system he controls.

7. Write a prayer of adoration expressing your awe at the majesty and splendor of God's holiness. Conclude your prayer by telling God what it means to you to be set apart to Him and from the world as a holy one (the literal meaning of *saint*).

THE CALL TO HOLINESS

IN THE BOOK of Isaiah, God is called *The Holy One of Israel* twenty-seven times. The Creator of the universe does not withdraw into His holiness and brood about how inferior His creatures are. He makes holiness part of His relationship with His people. By virtue of God's call, His people belong to Him, and He belongs to them. When God redeems sinners, His Holy Spirit calls them to become holy, too. The Spirit also enables us to obey that summons.

1. Read Isaiah 43:1–4, 10, 11, 21. In these verses *The Holy One of Israel* describes His call of His people to be holy. What do you observe in these verses regarding these three subjects?

The Holy One who calls (Is. 43:1, 3, 11)

The benefits of being called by the Holy One (Is. 43:2)

The responsibilities of being called by the Holy One (Is. 43:10, 21)

2. The prophet Ezekiel looked to the future and saw a day when God would send His Holy Spirit to make His new covenant effective with His people. Read Ezekiel 36:22–37. In this passage, what is the role of the Holy Spirit in calling the people of God to holiness?

3. Meditate quietly on your history with *The Holy One of Israel*. From what sins and disasters has He rescued you? What do you think your life would be like if *The Holy One of Israel* had not called you? How is the Holy Spirit renewing your heart?

Heart Sounds

A TRUE LOVE TO GOD MUST BEGIN WITH A DELIGHT IN HIS HOLINESS AND NOT WITH A DELIGHT IN ANY OTHER ATTRIBUTE; FOR NO OTHER ATTRIBUTE IS TRULY LOVELY WITHOUT THIS.

—Jonathan Edwards

4. Circle the letter of the statement that best expresses your previous attitude toward the notion that God would call you to holiness? If you choose *f. Other*, summarize your attitude in the space provided.

    a. I'd carry around a big Bible, preferably a chain reference edition, to bash people with.

    b. I'd have little in common with almost everyone around me, so I'd be lonely.

    c. I'd regularly perform miracles and speak in tongues.

    d. I'd know the peace and joy of living in harmony with the heart and mind of God.

    e. I'd walk around with a face so long I could eat olives right from the bottle.

    f. Other:

5. Perhaps the most challenging call to holiness in the New Testament is 1 Peter 1:13–19. Peter based his call on an important command in Leviticus: *You shall be holy, for I the LORD your God am holy* (Lev. 19:2). Read the passage in 1 Peter and write your thoughts in response to these questions.

In context, what did Peter have in mind when he used the term *holy*?

In this passage, what things are the opposites of holiness?

What can you conclude about holiness from the price of your redemption?

6. Spend a few minutes pondering each of these interpretations of *Be holy, for I am holy*. To what extent do you think each captures an aspect of Peter's meaning? If some are completely wrong, what's wrong with them?

Be holy in exactly the same way I am holy.

Be holy for the reason that I am holy.

Be holy through association with that which is holy.

Be holy out of fear of judgment by a holy God.

7. Number the reasons for holiness in item 6 from 1 to 4, with 1 being the strongest motivator and 4 being the weakest in terms of how you respond to them. Why do your first and second reasons for holiness appeal to you so much?

8. Identify someone in your family, church, small group, or circle of friends that you could tell what you learned from your call to holiness. Write his/her name and a time when you could do this. Jot down three or four main ideas you would like to share.

A New Song

Holy Father, show me your glory. Dazzle me with the brilliance of Your majesty. Burn away the dross of my soul and make me pure. Let Your holiness be the flame that melts my heart and tempers my spirit with holy resolve. Burnish my life until it reflects back to You the light that is Your own. When I can bear Your image thus, I will be my own true self at last and join the chorus singing, "Holy, holy, holy, Lord God Almighty." In Jesus' name. Amen.

THE BEAUTY OF HOLINESS

Some churches that associate themselves with the holiness movement build simple, functional buildings that have little ornamentation. Someone might conclude that holiness is austere in appearance and severe in behavior. The Bible, however, presents holiness as a beautiful quality of life, an ornament that draws observers to itself. Most holiness churches distinguish clearly between the people who comprise the church and the building in which the church meets. A beautiful building has nothing to do with holiness, but beautiful lives do.

1.   Write down the name of a person whose life attracted you to trust Jesus as Savior or to commit yourself fully to Him as Lord?

2.   As you think of this person's character, what did holiness—devotion to Christ and purity of life—have to do with his or her beauty of life?

3.   Read David's prayer on the occasion of the ark of the covenant arriving in Jerusalem recorded in 1 Chronicles 16:23–30. Also read Jehoshaphat's instructions to the choir accompanying his army found in 2 Chronicles 20:20–22.

Why do you think David envisioned *the beauty of holiness* (1 Chr. 16:29) causing the whole earth to tremble before the Lord?

How did King Jehoshaphat connect *the beauty of holiness* (2 Chr. 20:21) with the strength and protection of the Lord?

Grace Notes

The Pilgrims who landed on Plymouth Rock in 1620 and founded Plymouth Colony had separated from the Church of England to pursue holiness away from the politics and worldliness of a state church. They were not Puritans, dedicated to the reform of the Church of England. Puritans dressed in black, opposed theatrical entertainment, and gained a reputation—not truly deserved—for being killjoys. Their reputation has spilled over through the years onto the Pilgrims. If they had them, Pilgrims wore colorful clothes on glad occasions. They accepted the theater. They promoted loving family life in surprisingly frank language. The Pilgrims starved to death during early severe winters, and they never got free from debt to their colony financiers. But the Pilgrims cared more for the lives of beautiful holiness than they did for material success. It's a shame history books lump them together with the Puritans who later settled the Bay Colony around Boston.

4. *The beauty of holiness* should be the crown jewel of the virtues that adorn the life of a fully-devoted follower of Jesus Christ. In Isaiah 28, the prophet described the tribe of Ephraim—the leading tribe of the northern kingdom of Israel—in unflattering terms because they have adorned themselves with a different "crown jewel." Read Isaiah 28:1–6 where the prophet describes Ephraim, the judgment awaiting them, and their future revival.

With what negative spiritual quality did the tribe of Ephraim "crown" itself (Is. 28:1a, 3)?

What quality of their land were the Ephraimites depending on for security (Is. 28:1b, 4)?

In the future, with what would the Ephraimites "crown" themselves (Is. 28:5)? Why (28:6)?

5. Which of the following best expresses the worldly "crown" with which you are tempted to adorn your life?

   a. I am so ready to join Mensa and display my mental prowess.

   b. My 401k is bigger than your 401k.

   c. Move over, beautiful people.

   d. I have power, and I know how to use it.

   e. Everybody loves me!

   f. Other:

6. Spend a few minutes meditating on the beauty of holiness. Then write a letter to God. Choose the title you address Him with to capture the mood of what you want to say. Confess the cheap substitutes you have allowed to be crowned in your life in place of *the beauty of holiness*. Then open your heart and talk with the Lord about whatever you need or want, to beautify your life with holiness.

Listen to the Spirit

His divine power has given to us all things that pertain to life and godliness, through the knowledge of Him who called us by glory and virtue, by which have been given to us exceedingly great and precious promises, that through these you may be partakers of the divine nature, having escaped the corruption that is in the world through lust. But also for this very reason, giving all diligence, add to your faith virtue, to virtue knowledge, to knowledge self-control, to self-control perseverance, to perseverance godliness, to godliness brotherly kindness, and to brotherly kindness love. For if these things are yours and abound, you will be neither barren nor unfruitful in the knowledge of our Lord Jesus Christ.

—2 Peter 1:3–8

7. List below four aspects of God's holiness that you consider "beautiful." Each of the next four days, spend a few moments at the start of your prayer time imagining God "crowned" in majesty with one of these qualities.

Things I find beautiful about God

    a.

    b.

    c.

    d.

DAY 4 — PURIFICATION AND HOLINESS

God's holiness sets Him apart from all of His creatures—angelic, human, and animal. Some non-Christian religions with a starkly transcendental god take on a note of fatalism because their deity is indifferent to people. Such a god cannot care for insignificant humans. The God of the Bible, in the beauty of His holiness, commits Himself to making His worshipers holy, too. He forgives our sins through the substitutionary atonement of His Son's death on the Cross. He sanctifies us through the ministry of the indwelling Holy Spirit. For the rest of our lives, through occasional crisis experiences and daily gracious encounters, our heavenly Father is conforming us, His adopted children, into the image of His only begotten Son.

Listen to the Spirit

We learn about God by comparing Him to our human fathers. Sometimes that comparison is positive. "God is like my father in the sense that . . . ." Sometimes the comparison is negative. "My father was not effective in . . . . God will never fail me like that. Instead, He will . . . ."

Perhaps you grew up apart from your father. You don't have to be at a loss about what a good father is like. Paul wrote, *I bow my knees to the Father of our Lord Jesus Christ, from whom the whole family in heaven and earth is named* (Eph. 3:14, 15). In the end, we don't get a full picture of God by remembering our human fathers. We get a full picture of an ideal human father by studying God's relationship to Jesus, and to us His adopted children. Don't despair over faulty human relationships. Rejoice over your gracious, loving relationship with your Abba Father.

1. Read Hebrews 12:5–11. The author reasoned from Proverbs 3:11, 12 that chastening is one of God's tools for making us holy (Heb. 12:10). Chastening is a parent's discipline or corrective punishment on a misbehaving child.

For what sorts of things do you think our heavenly Father disciplines us?

Why does the writer of Hebrews say we should be glad our heavenly Father disciplines us?

How can the chastening of God produce greater holiness in our lives?

2. What do you suppose Satan wants our attitude to be toward God's chastening in our lives so he can prevent the growth of holiness in our lives?

Insight

Chastening differs from judgment. Chastening is corrective discipline. God chastens believers in His role as heavenly Father. Chastening is an expression of God's love and mercy. Judgment is punishment. God passes sentence on sinners in His role as Judge. Judgment is an expression of God's righteousness and justice.

Suffering is another means God uses to purify our lives. Some suffering arises from the circumstances accompanying living in a fallen world. Natural disasters, wars, and accidents fall into this category. Other suffering results from our own folly or sin. I suffer if I foolishly borrow more money than I can repay. I suffer the consequences of lying or committing adultery. Friends, spouses, and families suffer the consequences in their relationships of pride, jealousy, anger, bitterness, and selfishness. Still other suffering comes to Christians in the form of persecution by unbelievers. The Bible says more regarding the third kind of suffering than the other two. Most Christians in the western world suffer more from circumstances, folly, and sin than from overt persecution.

3. What does each of these Scriptures say that God wants to achieve in your life through suffering?

Romans 5:3, 4

James 1:2–4

1 Peter 1:6, 7

1 Peter 4:1, 2

1 Peter 4:12–19

The following four exercises give you opportunity to reflect on your suffering and try to discern the fingerprints of God on them and on you. Take time to pray and ponder before responding. If you are not good at introspection, consider discussing these items with a friend, spouse, or spiritual leader and completing these at another time.

4. How have you experienced suffering as a result of living in a fallen world? How has God used this suffering to purify your character?

5. How have you experienced suffering as the consequences of your own folly or sin? How has God used this suffering to purify your character?

6. How have you experienced suffering as a result of persecution for your faith in Christ? How has God used this suffering to purify your character?

7. How are you suffering at present? What do you think God wants to accomplish in your life through this? How can you cooperate with Him?

8. Look back through the Bible passages in item 3. Note and list the positive emotional and spiritual states promised to those who respond well to suffering. How do you think it possible that God produces qualities so good in our hearts through experiences so unpleasant in our lives?

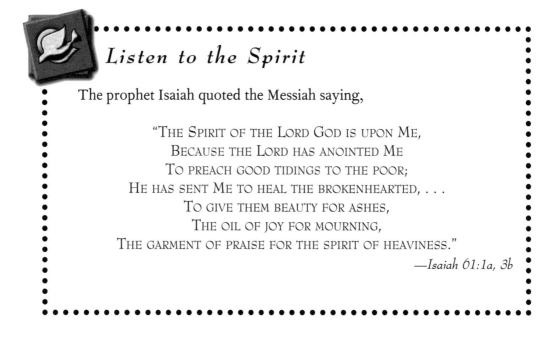

Listen to the Spirit

The prophet Isaiah quoted the Messiah saying,

> "THE SPIRIT OF THE LORD GOD IS UPON ME,
> BECAUSE THE LORD HAS ANOINTED ME
> TO PREACH GOOD TIDINGS TO THE POOR;
> HE HAS SENT ME TO HEAL THE BROKENHEARTED, . . .
> TO GIVE THEM BEAUTY FOR ASHES,
> THE OIL OF JOY FOR MOURNING,
> THE GARMENT OF PRAISE FOR THE SPIRIT OF HEAVINESS."
>
> —*Isaiah 61:1a, 3b*

HUMILITY AND HOLINESS

Back on Day 1, we said that holiness is an irreducibly fundamental idea when we talk about God. The splendor and majesty of His Being defy analysis and description. They overwhelm us and produce awe. From the human side, humility appears to be the irreducibly fundamental quality for interacting with God's holiness. We have no inherent splendor or majesty that corresponds to God's. We don't become holy by matching up with God strength for strength. We match up our weakness against His strength. Nobody looks God in the eye and says, "Here I am. Aren't You impressed?" Instead, afraid to raise our eyes to His holiness, we bow before God, confess our sins, and plead for forgiveness on the basis of Jesus' death in our place.

Surprisingly, God delights in exalting those who humble themselves. Then again, it's not so surprising. Humility is the path Jesus followed all the way to the Cross. From there, the Father exalted the Son to His right hand in heaven. All who follow Jesus down the path of humility find exaltation awaiting them—holiness of character in this life and eternal glory in the life to come.

1. Moses was discouraged after he came down from Sinai with the tablets of the Ten Commandments and found the Israelites worshiping a golden calf. He wrestled in his spirit with the Lord about continuing to lead the people, because God planned to withdraw His presence and send an angel as a substitute guide (Ex. 33:1–6, 12–16). The Lord relented and said He would accompany Israel the rest of the way to the Promised Land (33:17).

Moses asked one more favor of the Lord to fortify him for the daunting task of leading Israel. What was it (Ex. 33:18)?

How did Moses experience the holy glory of the Lord on the slopes of Mt. Sinai (Ex. 33:19–23)?

Moses' glimpse of God's holy glory is recorded prior to his lengthy stay on Mt. Sinai to receive the second set of tablets containing the Ten Commandments (Ex. 34). His vision of God in the cleft of the rock may have been a separate event, or it may have been the highlight of his encounters with the Lord on Sinai during that extended visit. In support of the latter view, Exodus 34:5–7 has many similarities to 33:19. How did Moses respond to his repeated exposure to the holy glory of God (Ex. 34:8)?

How did Abraham (Gen. 17:3), Ezekiel (Ezek. 1:28c; 3:23), Paul (Acts 9:4, 8), and John (Rev. 1:17) all react to visions of the holy glory of God?

What was the effect on Moses of being in the presence of the holy glory of God on Mt. Sinai for an extended time (Ex. 34:29–35)?

2. A crisis drove Moses to long for a glimpse of God's holiness more than anything else. He knew he couldn't go on as Israel's leader without a fresh vision of God's holiness to expand his spiritual depth and stamina. Reflect for a few moments on what has motivated you in the past and what motivates you in the present to seek fresh visions of the holiness of God. Record your thoughts below.

In the past

In the present

Heart Sounds

FOR THUS SAYS THE HIGH AND LOFTY ONE
WHO INHABITS ETERNITY, WHOSE NAME IS HOLY:
"I DWELL IN THE HIGH AND HOLY PLACE,
WITH HIM WHO HAS A CONTRITE AND HUMBLE SPIRIT,
TO REVIVE THE SPIRIT OF THE HUMBLE,
AND TO REVIVE THE HEART OF THE CONTRITE ONES."
—*Isaiah 57:15*

3. For a long time Moses' face reflected the holy glory of God seen on Mt. Sinai. Initially he veiled his glowing face because the Israelites were afraid of it (Ex. 34:30). After a while, Moses' motive for wearing the veil changed. What was his new motive (2 Cor. 3:7, 13) and what does this imply about Moses' spirit of humility?

4. Read 2 Corinthians 3:2–18 to see how Paul contrasted the transformation of believers in Jesus with the transformation Moses experienced on Mt. Sinai.

   Who reveals the holy glory of God to us (2 Cor. 3:3, 6, 8, 17, 18)?

   What are the necessary ingredients for progressive, uninterrupted transformation of our lives to conform to the holy glory of God (2 Cor. 3:16–18)?

5. Jesus is our example of humility in the presence of God the Father. Read Philippians 2:5–11.

How did Jesus progressively lower Himself in relation to His Father (2:6–8)?

How did the Father glorify the Son in response to His humility (2:9–11)?

6.   We do not experience the holy glory Jesus does as the divine Savior of the world. Neither does our humility affect the salvation of sinners. But the Holy Spirit will transform us progressively into the glorious image of our Lord if we submit to the purification process. Our humility before God's holy glory makes us soft, eager clay in the Spirit's hands. As you pray to encounter the transforming holiness of God, how can each of these express your humility before Him?

Your posture

Your forms of address to God

Emphasis on adoration in your prayers

The things you ask God for in your prayers

Grace Notes

In 1415, John Huss was burned at the stake in Constance, Switzerland. After he stood in the flames chanting hymns, he uttered three final words:

"O sancta simplicitas!"

"O holy simplicity!"

Death licked at Huss. Unimportant things dropped from the eye of his spirit. Everything became clear. Everything became one thing—one holy thing.

When in the course of our busy lives, we have face-to-face moments with God, unimportant things drop from sight. Everything becomes clear. Everything becomes one thing—one holy thing. And the Spirit transforms us from glory to glory, another step closer to His holy image.

CHAPTER 2

SPIRIT-FILLED WORSHIP

Right now—*right this minute*—something glorious is happening in heaven. It's been going on from eternity past and it will never, ever end. It's called worship, and thousands of years ago, the prophet Isaiah was granted a glimpse into the splendor of worship in heaven. "In the year that King Uzziah died, I saw the Lord sitting on a throne, high and lifted up, and the train of His robe filled the temple. Above it stood two seraphim; each one had six wings; with two he covered his face, with two he covered his feet, and with two he flew. And one cried to another and said: "Holy, holy, holy is the Lord of hosts; the whole earth is full of His glory!" (Is. 6:1–3) And you may know what happened to Isaiah. He was "undone". Worshiping in the presence of God will do that to a person.

But Isaiah was not the only one who saw into the heavenly realm. John the apostle made an observation of his own in Revelation 4:9–11. "Whenever the living creatures give glory and honor and thanks to Him who sits on the throne, who lives forever and ever, the twenty-four elders fall down before Him who sits on the throne and worship Him who lives forever and ever, and cast their crowns before the throne, saying: 'You are worthy, O Lord, to receive glory and honor and power; for You created all things, and by Your will they exist and were created.'" This is the heart of worship, that the Lord is worthy. He is worthy enough for twenty-four elders to take the crowns from their heads and throw them at His feet. And this goes on in heaven against the constant backdrop of angels who cannot stop crying, "Holy, holy, holy."

The God of the angels and the God of the elders, the God of Isaiah and the God of John—this is *our* God. This is the God we worship "in spirit and truth" (John 4:24). And as we worship, we are changed. Are you ready to worship Him?

DAY 1

THE PRIORITY OF WORSHIP

SOMETIMES YOU'LL HEAR preachers expound priorities for Christian living along this line: "When God saved you, why didn't He just take you up to heaven at that moment? Why did He leave you on earth?" The answer to that question is usually some form of evangelistic activity. The preacher might even say, "God didn't leave you on earth primarily to worship Him. You can do that better in heaven. The only thing you can't do better in heaven than on earth is proclaim the gospel to lost people because there won't be any lost people there."

This popular motivational device breaks Christianity into a set of tasks and ranks them on the basis of which "gets the job done." Christianity is a relationship between God and a community of redeemed sinners. Priority must be given to what strengthens the relationship between God and His adopted children. From that relationship flows God's kingdom-building activity in the world. Evangelism and all other forms of Christian service are the overflow of a worshipful heart into verbal and non-verbal witness. The fact that we will worship better in heaven than we can right now on earth does not diminish its foundational character.

1. Look at these Scripture passages, and identify the important activity over which worship took priority.

2 Chronicles 20:1, 20–22

Psalm 43

Matthew 26:6–13

Acts 2:1–14

All of the activities over which worship took priority were important. In some cases the activities flowed from worship or immediately followed worship. In all cases, worship established the relational context between God and man as the necessary spiritual basis for acts of service.

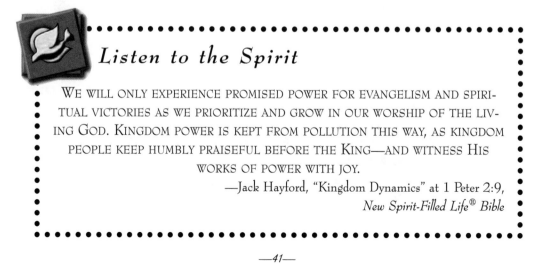

Listen to the Spirit

WE WILL ONLY EXPERIENCE PROMISED POWER FOR EVANGELISM AND SPIRITUAL VICTORIES AS WE PRIORITIZE AND GROW IN OUR WORSHIP OF THE LIVING GOD. KINGDOM POWER IS KEPT FROM POLLUTION THIS WAY, AS KINGDOM PEOPLE KEEP HUMBLY PRAISEFUL BEFORE THE KING—AND WITNESS HIS WORKS OF POWER WITH JOY.

—Jack Hayford, "Kingdom Dynamics" at 1 Peter 2:9,
New Spirit-Filled Life® Bible

2. Read and meditate on Psalm 42. Answer the following questions from your reflection.

    a. The psalmist was physically separated from the temple of the Lord in Jerusalem (42:6), so he could not engage in worship as prescribed in the Law of Moses. What things intrude into your life and prevent you from giving worship its place of priority?

    b. What was the psalmist's emotional reaction to worship deprivation (42:3a, 5a, 6a, 11a)?

    c. How did worship deprivation affect the psalmist's ability to cope with opposition (42:3b, 10)?

    d. How does worship deprivation impair your inner resources to deal with stress and opposition?

    e. What was the psalmist's first step in dealing with worship deprivation (42:4, 6b)?

f. What resulted from the psalmist's remembrance of prior worship experiences (42:1, 2)?

g. What was the psalmist's final emotional state as he reflected on worship (42:11b)?

h. List three of the best worship experiences you remember from your past. What emotional response do you have to the memory of each of them?

i. What would you like to hope for as the result of giving worship of God a higher priority in your life?

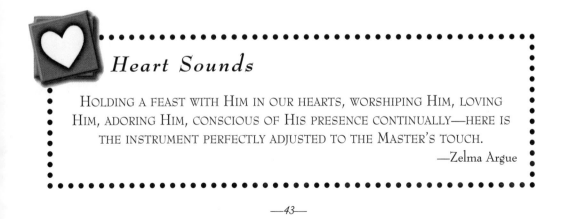

Heart Sounds

HOLDING A FEAST WITH HIM IN OUR HEARTS, WORSHIPING HIM, LOVING HIM, ADORING HIM, CONSCIOUS OF HIS PRESENCE CONTINUALLY—HERE IS THE INSTRUMENT PERFECTLY ADJUSTED TO THE MASTER'S TOUCH.

—Zelma Argue

3.   Undoubtedly the biggest obstacle to giving worship priority in our lives is making time in our busy schedules. Circle all of the items on the following list that squeeze your available time for worship.

1.   Work schedule exceeding forty hours a week.

2.   Time spent commuting to work.

3.   Kids' classes, sports, and clubs.

4.   Physical exercise regimen.

5.   Church leadership commitments.

6.   Bible studies and small groups.

7.   Hobbies and clubs.

8.   Golf, bowling, softball, basketball, or other sports activities.

9.   Hunting and fishing.

10.   Yard work and home maintenance.

11.   Television.

12.   Internet usage.

13.   Shopping.

14.   Arts and crafts.

4.   Put a star by the items you circled above that you cannot easily change. Put a double star by those you can readily do something about. Write an action plan for freeing more time to engage in private worship of God.

5. Where would you be most likely to have a quiet place to engage in worship (home, office, in the park, etc.)? At what time of day would you most likely find time to worship?

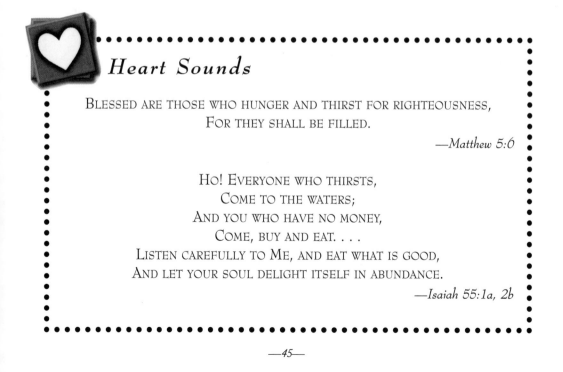

Heart Sounds

BLESSED ARE THOSE WHO HUNGER AND THIRST FOR RIGHTEOUSNESS,
FOR THEY SHALL BE FILLED.

—Matthew 5:6

HO! EVERYONE WHO THIRSTS,
COME TO THE WATERS;
AND YOU WHO HAVE NO MONEY,
COME, BUY AND EAT. . . .
LISTEN CAREFULLY TO ME, AND EAT WHAT IS GOOD,
AND LET YOUR SOUL DELIGHT ITSELF IN ABUNDANCE.

—Isaiah 55:1a, 2b

THE HEART OF WORSHIP

WORSHIP IS NOT a matter of technique; it's a matter of relationship. Worship is not a matter of asking God to do things for us; it's a matter of expressing wonder and gratitude to Him. Worship is an area of Christian living in which the doctrine of the Trinity is important. Worship involves adoring Father, Son, and Holy Spirit for who They are and what They do for the benefit of all and for you. Worship is intensely personal. It springs from your heart. Worship is intensely interpersonal. Its vitality depends on the quality of your fellowship with Father, Son, and Spirit.

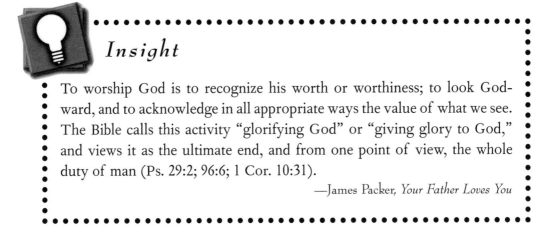

Insight

To worship God is to recognize his worth or worthiness; to look Godward, and to acknowledge in all appropriate ways the value of what we see. The Bible calls this activity "glorifying God" or "giving glory to God," and views it as the ultimate end, and from one point of view, the whole duty of man (Ps. 29:2; 96:6; 1 Cor. 10:31).

—James Packer, *Your Father Loves You*

1. Which of the following responses best completes this statement for you? Coming into this study, I thought the heart of worship was

    a.   A praise song title.

    b.   When they took the offering at church.

    c.   Praying through my prayer list.

    d.   Personal Bible study.

    e.   Praying in tongues.

    f.   Focused adoration of God.

    g.   Other:

2.   On the following continuum, how would you rate your worship of God? In the space below the continuum, think on paper what you would like your private worship to be.

1	2	3	4	5	6	7	8	9	10
Awful		So-so		Showing		Exciting			Awesome
				Improvement		At Times			

2.   In Ephesians 1:3–14, the apostle Paul praised the three Persons of the Godhead. Verses 3–6 praise God the Father. Verses 7–12 marvel at the work of God the Son. Verses 13, 14 exalt God the Holy Spirit. Read this biblical doxology slowly two or three times. Open your heart and spirit to the grandeur of Paul's glorification of God. Then answer the following questions.

    a.   What is the overall reason Paul gave for worshiping God (Eph. 1:3)?

    b.   Paul concluded his worship of each Person of the Godhead with a similar phrase. What was it (Eph. 1:6, 12, 14)?

c.   For what glories about God the Father did Paul bless Him (Eph. 1:3–6)?

d.   For what glories about God the Son did Paul bless Him (Eph. 1:7–12)?

e.   For what glories about God the Holy Spirit did Paul bless Him (Eph. 1:13, 14)?

3.   From Ephesians 1:3–6 and other sources, what awe-inspiring truths about God the Father move you to worship Him?

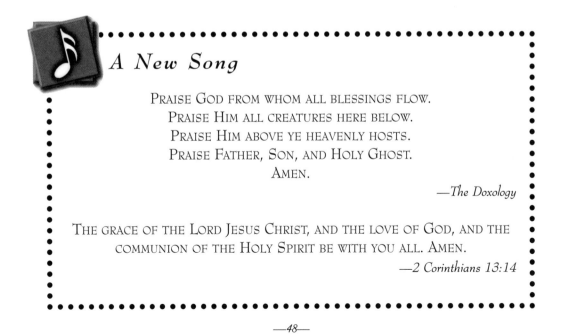

A New Song

PRAISE GOD FROM WHOM ALL BLESSINGS FLOW.
PRAISE HIM ALL CREATURES HERE BELOW.
PRAISE HIM ABOVE YE HEAVENLY HOSTS.
PRAISE FATHER, SON, AND HOLY GHOST.
AMEN.

—The Doxology

THE GRACE OF THE LORD JESUS CHRIST, AND THE LOVE OF GOD, AND THE COMMUNION OF THE HOLY SPIRIT BE WITH YOU ALL. AMEN.

—2 Corinthians 13:14

4. From Ephesians 1:7–12 and other sources, what awe-inspiring truths about God the Son move you to worship Him?

5. From Ephesians 1:13, 14 and other sources, what awe-inspiring truths about God the Holy Spirit move you to worship Him?

6. Consider your present worship. To which Person(s) of the Godhead do you need to pay more attention? How can you do this? How should you adjust the balance in your devotional time between praising God and asking Him to do stuff for you?

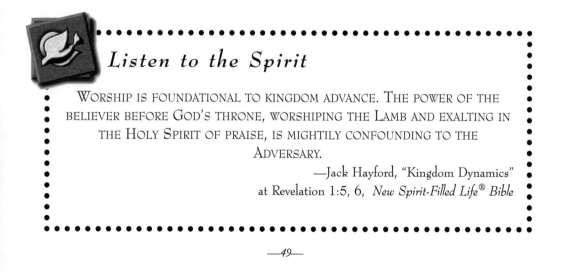

Listen to the Spirit

WORSHIP IS FOUNDATIONAL TO KINGDOM ADVANCE. THE POWER OF THE BELIEVER BEFORE GOD'S THRONE, WORSHIPING THE LAMB AND EXALTING IN THE HOLY SPIRIT OF PRAISE, IS MIGHTILY CONFOUNDING TO THE ADVERSARY.

—Jack Hayford, "Kingdom Dynamics"
at Revelation 1:5, 6, *New Spirit-Filled Life® Bible*

THE CONTENT OF WORSHIP

C. S. LEWIS WROTE IN *Reflections on the Psalms*, "I think we delight to praise what we enjoy because the praise not merely expresses but completes the enjoyment. It is not out of compliment that lovers keep on telling one another how beautiful they are; the delight is incomplete till it is expressed." Learning to worship means learning to praise aloud—and sometimes in the presence of others. We cannot praise God until we delight in Him and love Him. We can't do those things until we know Him intimately. We cannot know Him intimately until we spend time with Him.

Heart Sounds

Progress in the Christian life is exactly equal to the growing knowledge we gain of the Triune God in personal experience. And such experience requires a whole life devoted to it and plenty of time spent at the holy task of cultivating God. God can be known satisfactorily only as we devote time to Him. . . . There is no short cut to sanctity.

—A. W. Tozer, *The Roots of the Righteous*

Let's look at Psalms 95 and 96 to discover some components of biblical praise. These can guide us in evaluating our own praise and in planning how to improve it. In the process, we will discover how to spend time with God in ways that will both increase and express our delight in Him. To begin, read Psalms 95 and 96 twice. The first time read the two psalms quickly to get an impression of their content and impact. The second time, read them aloud, slowly and meditatively, looking for personal appeals and commands to praise the Lord. Let the following questions guide your response to these psalms.

1. What specific activities do the psalmists recommend for praising God (Ps. 95:1, 2, 6; 96:1–3, 7–10)?

2. What postures can you imagine assuming for each of the praise activities in item 1?

3. What titles or descriptions are given God in praise (Ps. 95:1, 3–5, 6, 7; 96:1–10)? What praise activity is connected with each of these?

4. Contrast the past response of God's people to Him (Ps. 95:8–11) with the future response of God's inanimate world to Him (Ps. 96:11–13). What mood or tone should this reality inject into your praise of God?

5. For what sort of things do these psalms suggest you should praise God?

6. From your own experience, for what additional matters should you praise God?

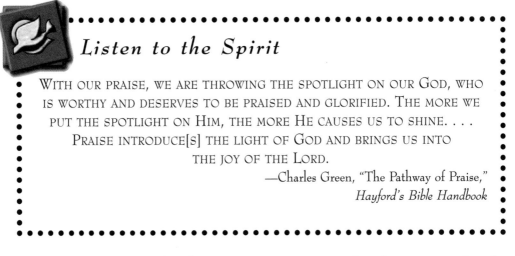

Listen to the Spirit

WITH OUR PRAISE, WE ARE THROWING THE SPOTLIGHT ON OUR GOD, WHO IS WORTHY AND DESERVES TO BE PRAISED AND GLORIFIED. THE MORE WE PUT THE SPOTLIGHT ON HIM, THE MORE HE CAUSES US TO SHINE. . . . PRAISE INTRODUCE[S] THE LIGHT OF GOD AND BRINGS US INTO THE JOY OF THE LORD.

—Charles Green, "The Pathway of Praise," *Hayford's Bible Handbook*

7. Make an action plan for incorporating praise of Father, Son, and Holy Spirit into your private worship of God. Jot down three praise elements you want to include in your devotional time next week. How will these alter the way you have conducted devotions in the past?

8. Make an action plan for incorporating praise of Father, Son, and Holy Spirit into your public worship of God. Jot down three praise elements you want to include in your public worship (You may already do some of these). How will these alter the way you have previously worshiped in public?

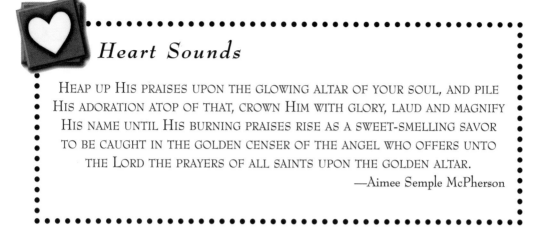

Heart Sounds

Heap up His praises upon the glowing altar of your soul, and pile His adoration atop of that, crown Him with glory, laud and magnify His name until His burning praises rise as a sweet-smelling savor to be caught in the golden censer of the angel who offers unto the Lord the prayers of all saints upon the golden altar.

—Aimee Semple McPherson

THE THRONE OF WORSHIP

EVERY NOW AND then you'll meet a skeptic who says, "What kind of God is this who needs yes-men and yes-women to gather around and tell Him how wonderful He is? If you worked for a boss like that, you'd hate him and think he was the most insecure or egotistical guy around. This worship thing shows God to be a bully or a weakling." The trouble with such a line of thinking is that it treats God as a "bigger human," greater only in degree. But God isn't a bigger, stronger, smarter me. He is totally Other. If I see Him as He is, I must bow in awe. There is no other response I can make. Worship of God by people is the normal, natural relationship between the two.

God doesn't need my worship to boost His ego or prove He's in charge. I need to worship to keep my spiritual equilibrium. To worship is to point the compass of my spirit due north and to say, "There lies the Way, the Truth, and the Life." Worship is a way of saying, "Lord, You are the King; I am Your subject. Yours is the kingdom. Your will be done on my little bit of earth, as it is in all of Your heaven."

God responds to such worship. Set up His throne in your life by praise and worship and He will show up to rule from that throne. Worship is not a "feel good" emotional release. It isn't a search for some altered consciousness through repeated physical movements, repeated mantra-like phrases, and self-hypnosis. Worship is facing God, wiping the world from my eyes, waiting until His glory comes into focus, and saying, "Yes! Yes! Yes!"

1. In light of the opening comments about worship, read the Lord's Prayer in Matthew 6:9–13. Write your thoughts about the significance of each of these opening lines of the prayer in terms of worship.

    Our Father in heaven,

Hallowed be Your name.

Your kingdom come.

Your will be done on earth as it is in heaven.

Listen to the Spirit

FEW PRINCIPLES ARE MORE ESSENTIAL TO OUR UNDERSTANDING THAN THIS ONE: THE <u>PRESENCE</u> OF GOD'S KINGDOM POWER IS DIRECTLY RELATED TO THE PRACTICE OF GOD'S <u>PRAISE</u>. THE VERB "ENTHRONED" INDICATES THAT WHEREVER GOD'S PEOPLE EXALT HIS NAME, HE IS READY TO MANIFEST HIS KINGDOM'S POWER IN THE WAY MOST APPROPRIATE TO THE SITUATION, AS HIS RULE IS INVITED TO INVADE OUR SETTING.

—Jack Hayford, "Kingdom Dynamics"
at Psalm 22:3, *New Spirit-Filled Life*® *Bible*

2. Read Psalm 22:3–5. In these verses, David asserted that God's throne is established by the praise of His people—past and present. David was counting on that spiritual reality as an antidote to the desperate situation in which he found himself.

   a. What was David's situation when he began to enthrone God with worship (Ps. 22:1, 2, 12–18)?

b. Identify the moment in Psalm 22:21 when David knew that God had taken His throne.

c. What happened to David's outlook when God was enthroned on his praise (Ps. 22:22–31)?

d. Which of your negative moods and attitudes could benefit from enthroning God with praise and worship?

e. In what crisis situations (past, present, or imagined) would enthroning God by means of worship and praise be a wise and godly option? How would it be of benefit?

A New Song

SING PRAISES TO THE LORD, WHO DWELLS IN ZION;
DECLARE HIS DEEDS AMONG THE PEOPLE.

—Psalm 9:11

3. In the space below, write a prayer of worship. As you write it, imagine the appropriate actions and postures. Include as many of these aspects of worship as you can. Adore the Father, Son, and Holy Spirit. Praise the mighty deeds of the triune God with song, shouts of joy, and testimony to everyone around. Kneel humbly before Him; lift holy hands to receive His presence and blessing. Crown Him King of your life and welcome Him to the throne of your praise.

A New Song

GOOD MORNING, HEAVENLY FATHER;
GOOD MORNING, LORD JESUS;
GOOD MORNING, HOLY SPIRIT.
HEAVENLY FATHER, I WORSHIP YOU AS THE CREATOR AND SUSTAINER OF
THE UNIVERSE.
LORD JESUS, I WORSHIP YOU, SAVIOR AND LORD OF THE WORLD.
HOLY SPIRIT, I WORSHIP YOU, SANCTIFIER OF THE PEOPLE OF GOD.
GLORY TO THE FATHER, AND TO THE SON, AND TO THE HOLY SPIRIT.
AS IT WAS IN THE BEGINNING, IS NOW, AND WILL BE FOREVER.
IN JESUS' NAME.
AMEN.

—John Stott, "A Prayer for the Day"

THE IMPACT OF WORSHIP

WORSHIP ISN'T FLATTERY of a vain deity as skeptics would say, and worship isn't a psychological gimmick to help worshipers reach an exalted emotional state that leaves them feeling good. Worship pierces the veil separating the finite physical world from the infinite spiritual realm. Worship recognizes, delights in, and responds in awe to the terrible majesty of the triune God. Worship builds a throne of praise for God to assume as King. That has to mean that the throne room of worship is the place where worshipers are most prepared to hear the King give His marching orders for that day or for the rest of their lives.

Listen to the Spirit

WE DO NOT MANIPULATE GOD, BUT ALIGN OURSELVES WITH THE GREAT KINGDOM TRUTH: HIS IS THE POWER, OURS IS THE PRIVILEGE (AND RESPONSIBILITY) TO WELCOME HIM INTO OUR WORLD—OUR PRIVATE, PRESENT WORLD OR THE CIRCUMSTANCES OF OUR SOCIETY.

—Jack Hayford, "Kingdom Dynamics"
at Psalm 22:3, *New Spirit-Filled Life® Bible*

After the prophet Elijah defeated 450 prophets of Baal in spiritual combat on the summit of Mount Carmel (1 Kin. 18:20–40), he faced a time of uncertainty and doubt in his personal life and in his ministry. It took a worship encounter with the Lord on Mount Sinai, where Moses earlier had seen the Lord and been transformed by Him (Chapter One, Day Five), to get Elijah's life and ministry back on track. Read 1 Kings 19:1–18. (If your time permits, begin your reading at 1 Kings 17:1).

1. What were the cause and the extent of Elijah's discouragement after his great victory at Mount Carmel (2 Kin. 19:1–4)?

2. How did the Lord prepare His prophet Elijah for a worship encounter that would impact his life (1 Kin. 19:5–8)?

3. Why do you think God wanted Elijah to fully express his discouragement before redirecting his life and ministry (1 Kin. 19:9, 10)?

4. Why do you think Elijah needed to meet God in a quiet voice rather than a power display at this point in his life (1 Kin. 19:11, 12)?

5. How did Elijah express His reverence of the Lord (1 Kin. 19:13)?

6. How did the Lord respond to Elijah's repetition of his self-pitying remark in verse 15 (1 Kin. 19:16–18)?

7. What new responsibility did the Lord give Elijah in each of these areas?

    The wider world (1 Kin: 19:15)

    His community (1 Kin. 19:16a)

    His spiritual community (1 Kin. 19:16b)

8. How do you think a worship encounter with God prepared Elijah to receive and obey these commands of the Lord, with all the heavy responsibility involved in them, even though none of his complaints was answered?

Grace Notes

I have found it easy to obtain the presence of God. He desires to be more present to us than we are to seek Him. He desires to give Himself to us more readily than we are to receive Him.

—Madame Jeanne Guyon

9. Circle the letters of the following statements that you have found true of your worship encounters with God.

   a. I have sensed God making clear decisions that had puzzled me before.

   b. God has directed me to share Christ with some specific person.

   c. God has given me peace about a troubling situation.

   d. I have heard the audible voice of God.

   e. I have seen a vision that gave me guidance.

   f. God has directed me to do something I never considered before.

   g. Other:

10. We should expect the commands of the King from His throne of praise to involve His kingdom rule in our lives and our world. That was certainly Elijah's experience. Our tendency is to want Him to speak to us about the things we want, rather than the things He wants. What can you do in your worship to make sure you are yielding to the will of your King instead of putting words in His mouth? Think about this for a while before recording your thoughts.

11. Glance back through the five studies dealing with Spirit-filled worship. Pause briefly and ask the Holy Spirit to guide you into the truth about how He wants to enhance your worship to honor God and advance His kingdom in your life. What do you think are the main issues and lessons about worship on which the Spirit wants you to focus?

CHAPTER 3

SPIRIT-FILLED KINGDOM LIVING

This holy God you've found new delight in worshiping intends to set up His kingdom on this earth. We know that, but we tend to think of God's kingdom as a someday and somewhere thing. However, a big part of renewing our minds is learning to think of God's kingdom as a today and right here kind of thing. Didn't Jesus teach us to pray, "Your kingdom come. Your will be done on earth as it is in heaven"? Of course He did. But what does "Your kingdom come" really mean? In simplest terms, it is a cry for the rule and reign of King Jesus to be exalted over every aspect of our lives and for the ways of God to govern our daily walk on earth.

As we commit and submit to the transforming work of the Holy Spirit, we become kingdom people, dedicated to our King and serving Him with passion. Even though our everyday activities may not change, our motivation for doing them will change as we realize that we are fueled by a desire for our lives to be an offering to the King we adore. Our attitudes change as we realize that we are working and living "As unto the Lord". Are you ready for that kind of kingdom life?

PEOPLE OF THE KINGDOM

PEOPLE OF THE kingdom of God have, in a sense, dual citizenship. We live in this world and concern ourselves with the politics, economics, social issues, family concerns, and personal issues arising from life on this fallen planet. At the same time, we care deeply about the expansion of God's kingdom across national boundaries, without regard to any nation's interests. We believe that kingdom treasures are not measured in dollars, yen, or euros. We know all nations can be brothers and sisters in Jesus. In the final analysis, biblical values say we are citizens of the invisible kingdom of God and pilgrims and strangers in the very country where we were born.

It's no wonder that some nations that do not have centuries of Christian cultural heritage fear Christians may be a subversive element in their societies. It takes a Christian cultural perspective to realize that the expansion of kingdom values in any social system produces stability, order, and mutual concern among its citizenry. What are people of the kingdom like?

1. On Day 4 in Chapter 2 of this workbook, you reflected on the first four lines of the Lord's Prayer in Matthew 6:9, 10. Read those verses again and review your responses in that portion of "Spirit-Filled Worship." How do these verses function as a "pledge of allegiance" to the kingdom of God?

Insight

In Colossians 1:13, "the power of darkness" is contrasted with "the kingdom of the Son of His love." "Power" translates the Greek noun *exousia*, and here refers to the power exercised by a ruler, namely Satan. "Power" takes on the formal sense of "domain." The NIV translates the verse like this: *For he has rescued us from the dominion of darkness and brought us into the kingdom of the Son he loves.*

2. Read Colossians 1:13; Hebrews 11:9, 10, 13–16; and 1 Peter 2:11, 12. What do you learn about the following topics?

The character of earthly and heavenly kingdoms (Col. 1:13)

The pilgrim nature of life on earth (Heb. 11:9, 10, 13–16)

The moral struggle of dual citizenship in earthly and heavenly kingdoms (1 Pet. 2:11, 12)

3. In what ways are we to represent the kingdom of God on earth according to these passages of Scripture?

2 Corinthians 5:14-20

Ephesians 6:10–20

1 Peter 2:13–17

4. In the future, the kingdom of God will be established on the earth with Christ as its King. Presently, the King is in heaven at the right hand of His Father. Therefore, *our citizenship is in heaven, from which we eagerly wait for the Savior, the Lord Jesus Christ* (Phil. 3:20). When the King comes to earth, our citizenship will be transferred to the New Jerusalem (Rev. 21:9—22:5). In the meantime, Paul advised, *Seek those things which are above, where Christ is sitting at the right hand of God* (Col. 3:1). What heavenly subjects do you think you should ponder in order to represent the King well on earth? What heavenly qualities do you need to exhibit to be a good ambassador?

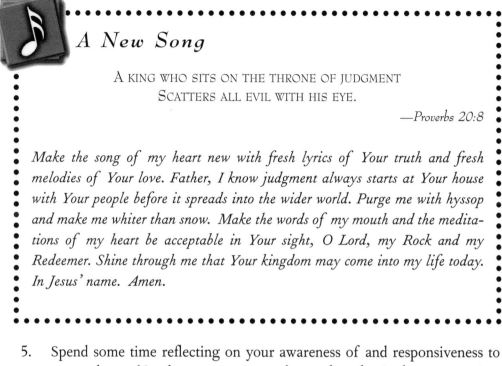

A New Song

A KING WHO SITS ON THE THRONE OF JUDGMENT
SCATTERS ALL EVIL WITH HIS EYE.

—Proverbs 20:8

Make the song of my heart new with fresh lyrics of Your truth and fresh melodies of Your love. Father, I know judgment always starts at Your house with Your people before it spreads into the wider world. Purge me with hyssop and make me whiter than snow. Make the words of my mouth and the meditations of my heart be acceptable in Your sight, O Lord, my Rock and my Redeemer. Shine through me that Your kingdom may come into my life today. In Jesus' name. Amen.

5.   Spend some time reflecting on your awareness of and responsiveness to your role as a kingdom person. Record your thoughts in these categories:

Ways in which I'm too much "at home" in this world

Ways I do pretty well in welcoming the kingdom of God

Ways I want to become a better pilgrim, citizen of heaven, ambassador, or spiritual warrior (Pick one)

THE KINGDOM WITHIN YOU

HOW CAN THE kingdom of God become more than an abstraction—a high-sounding synonym for doing the will of God? Jesus provides us with the clues we need for answering this question in His words and in the pattern of His life. A group of Pharisees once came to Jesus and asked Him for a checklist of things to look for to recognize the arrival of the kingdom of God (Luke 17:20). Jesus replied that the kingdom of God will never be brought in by means of end-time charts and prophecy conferences. *"The kingdom of God is within you,"* Jesus said (17:21).

Heart Sounds

"Something more than the sun, greater than the light, is coming—nonetheless surely coming that it is long upon the road."
—George MacDonald, *Phantastes*

The kingdom of God has been occupying the territory of human hearts for two thousand years. It is coming to you today in the reign of King Jesus through the power of the Holy Spirit who lives within you as the seal of your heavenly inheritance. Enthrone the King in your heart on your praises and let Him reign from there.

1. When Jesus returns—whether His arrival be today, next year, or in the distant future—He will establish a literal kingdom. To understand the spiritual one that He wants to set up in each born-again believer, it's necessary to look briefly at the future, physical kingdom. Read Zechariah 9:9, 10. What do you learn from this passage about each of the following?

The King

The Realm

The Reign

2. Zechariah 9:10 quotes Psalm 72:8, a verse from a psalm King Solomon wrote. Read Psalm 72:1–17. (The final three verses are the doxology and summary of the second book of the Psalter, Psalms 42—72.) What do you learn from Solomon's psalm about the future reign of Christ on earth?

3. Between the time Jesus ascended to heaven after His Crucifixion and Resurrection and the time He will return to establish the kingdom of God on earth, His kingdom lies within His people. If Jesus is your Savior, His

realm encompasses all of your life that you surrender to His authority. Read Colossians 3:1–4. How does the apostle Paul say we prepare our hearts and minds for the reign of Jesus?

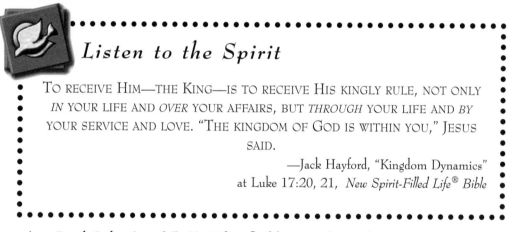

Listen to the Spirit

To receive Him—the King—is to receive His kingly rule, not only *IN* your life and *OVER* your affairs, but *THROUGH* your life and *BY* your service and love. "The kingdom of God is within you," Jesus said.

—Jack Hayford, "Kingdom Dynamics"
at Luke 17:20, 21, *New Spirit-Filled Life® Bible*

4.   Read Colossians 3:5–11. What fleshly attitudes and practices stand in the way of Christ's reign in our lives? Which of these are significant problems for you? How do you see them diminishing the kingdom of God within you?

5. Read Colossians 3:12–17. What are the qualities that the reign of Christ in your life will produce? Underline the qualities you need, but have not "put on" through the power of God's Spirit. Circle the ones that are strong or are emerging as strong in your life. What do these strengths and weaknesses suggest about the kingdom of God within you?

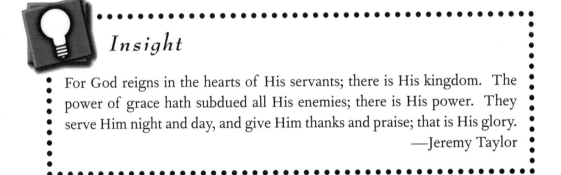

Insight

For God reigns in the hearts of His servants; there is His kingdom. The power of grace hath subdued all His enemies; there is His power. They serve Him night and day, and give Him thanks and praise; that is His glory.

—Jeremy Taylor

6. Circle the letter of the statement that best reflects the state of the kingdom of God within you. In the space following the options, write a prayer to God opening the "borders" of your life, giving Him access to every part of it. Be specific.

    a. God owns my life but the borders have been closed against Him.

    b. God has control of the "religious" parts of my life, but I keep control of the everyday parts.

    c. I thought I had surrendered my life to God's control, but there are a surprising number of areas I have kept from Him.

    d. I have surrendered my entire life to God in the past. I need to update my commitment to keep it fresh.

    e. To the best of my knowledge and ability, God reigns in all my life.

DAY 3 — CHARACTER AND THE KINGDOM

THE INTRODUCTION TO this workbook suggested that "the Christian life can be summarized as giving all that I know of myself to all that I know of God." Contemplating the kingdom of God invites us to consider ourselves—our character—and decide whether the offerings we are presenting to God satisfy our desire to please Him.

When we accepted Christ as Savior, we became His possession by right of purchase. He ransomed us by His death on the Cross. At the practical, daily level, bits and pieces of our lives must be consciously wrestled away from habit-based influence of the flesh and consecrated to the full lordship of Jesus. If your life

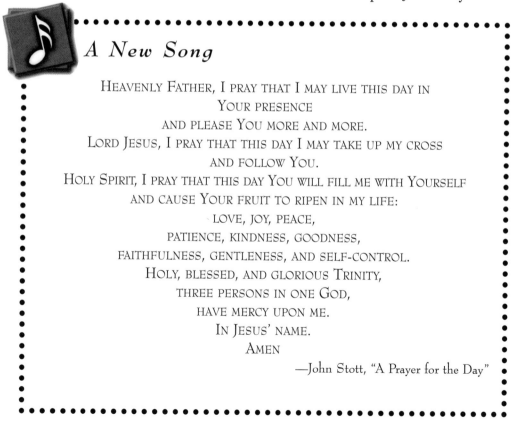

A New Song

HEAVENLY FATHER, I PRAY THAT I MAY LIVE THIS DAY IN
YOUR PRESENCE
AND PLEASE YOU MORE AND MORE.
LORD JESUS, I PRAY THAT THIS DAY I MAY TAKE UP MY CROSS
AND FOLLOW YOU.
HOLY SPIRIT, I PRAY THAT THIS DAY YOU WILL FILL ME WITH YOURSELF
AND CAUSE YOUR FRUIT TO RIPEN IN MY LIFE:
LOVE, JOY, PEACE,
PATIENCE, KINDNESS, GOODNESS,
FAITHFULNESS, GENTLENESS, AND SELF-CONTROL.
HOLY, BLESSED, AND GLORIOUS TRINITY,
THREE PERSONS IN ONE GOD,
HAVE MERCY UPON ME.
IN JESUS' NAME.
AMEN

—John Stott, "A Prayer for the Day"

could be compared to the map of a country, Jesus owns every square mile of it—every river, hill, field, village, and city. But He only occupies each part of that country by means of the Holy Spirit as it is opened to Him.

Jesus spent three years preparing His disciples to be kingdom people who would give the Holy Spirit full access to their lives. Look at the following portions of the Sermon on the Mount to see what He had to say to them—and to us—about the quality of character He expects of kingdom people.

1. What did Jesus identify as the basic attitude that should characterize kingdom people (Matt. 5:3)?

2. Circle the letter of the statement that best expresses your concept of humility. In the space that follows, describe how you would like to grow in humility.

    a. I'm a worthless nobody whom people walk on.

    b. If they only knew how much potential I have, everyone would be impressed, but I mustn't say anything. That would be prideful.

    c. If I can behave in a humble manner, everyone will respect me.

    d. I feel good about my gifts and abilities. I'm happy to use them for God's glory.

    e. I'm God's gift to my church and family, and everybody knows it.

3. What is the only other beatitude that Jesus connected with possessing the kingdom of heaven (Matt. 5:10)? What connections can you imagine between poverty of spirit and strength to face persecution for the sake of righteousness?

4. Circle the letters of the following forms of persecution for your faith you have endured.

   a. Physical assault.

   b. Verbal abuse.

   c. Ridicule.

   d. Social isolation.

   e. Passed over for promotion at work/opportunities at school.

   f. Loss of friendship.

   g. Other:

5. What kinds of responses to your persecution would classify as shining like a light or being a preservative like salt (Matt. 5:13–16)?

6. The scribes and Pharisees of Jesus' day based their claims of righteousness on careful observance of the letter of the law. In the Sermon on the Mount, Jesus based the righteousness of the kingdom of God on the heart attitudes that lay behind the laws of the Old Testament (Matt. 5:17–20). By temperament, are you a by-the-book person or a spirit-of-the-law person? What are the strengths and weaknesses of your kind of person? What reminders do you need from the Holy Spirit to keep you in balance?

Heart Sounds

We shall be judged according to our privileges, according to the light we have received, and the obedience we have rendered to it, not only outwardly but inwardly, according to our rebellion or submission to God; according to our loyalty and obedience to Him, in our hearts as well as in our lives.

—Catherine Booth

7. The Lord's Prayer is a prayer for the kingdom of God in our lives (Matt. 6:9–13). How does the Lord's Prayer differ in content and emphasis from most of your praying?

    How would your values have to change for your kingdom praying to become more like the Lord's Prayer?

8. Jesus taught that kingdom people value different things than worldly people and invest their wealth differently (Matt. 6:24–34). What steps do you need to take to give the kingdom of God greater priority over your material concerns? What is the biggest stumbling block you face to achieving this?

Grace Notes

John Wesley headed off to Oxford University at age 21. He was bright and handsome; he was snobbish and sarcastic. One night, he made fun of a poor university servant who had only one coat and no bed. The man was so relentlessly cheerful that he annoyed young Wesley, who sarcastically jibed, "And what else do you thank God for?"

The porter smiled and replied, "I thank Him that He has given me my life and being, a heart to love Him, and above all a constant desire to serve Him!" Wesley had the sense to be shamed and to remember the incident to his improvement.

—*Our Daily Bread*

9. If you were to compare your life to the map of a country, what are the pockets of territory you have resisted turning over to the King? Circle the letter(s) of the items on the following list that apply to you. Then spend some time in prayer talking with God about how you should handle these character issues. Record your impression of His answers to your prayer in the space below the list.

   a. My family.

   b. My career.

   c. My financial goals.

   d. A life-dominating habit.

   e. Anger.

   f. Unforgiveness.

   g. Anxiety.

   h. Other:

DAY 4   *THE SPIRIT AND THE KINGDOM*

EVERYONE WHO WANTS to live for the Lord and serve Him as a kingdom person must be *born of the Spirit* (John 3:5, 6). The kingdom of God in this age is a spiritual rather than a physical realm. Anyone who gets serious about the kingdom must be serious about relying on the Holy Spirit.

1. Jesus did not begin proclaiming the gospel of the kingdom of God until after His baptism by John the Baptist. What appears to have been the reason Jesus began His public ministry at that time (Luke 3:22; 4:1, 14–21)?

2. After Jesus' Crucifixion and Resurrection, He commissioned His disciples to take the gospel of the kingdom to all creatures. His disciples wanted to know if Jesus was ready to establish His physical kingdom (Acts 1:6). Jesus diverted attention from that question to a more important one. What is Jesus' concern for those who will proclaim the kingdom of God and live as its representatives (John 20:21, 22; Acts 1:5–8)?

3. Throughout the Book of Acts, the Holy Spirit played a key role in the spread of the gospel of the kingdom of God. Examine Acts 2:4; 4:8, 31; 9:17; 13:9 and summarize the Spirit's relationship to the messengers of the kingdom.

4.   Not only did the Spirit come on kingdom messengers in the Book of Acts to empower various moments of witness, but He maintained an ongoing presence in their lives. Examine Acts 6:3–5; 7:55–60; 11:22–26 and comment on the nature and affect of the Spirit's abiding presence.

Insight

There are two primary expressions for the filling of the Holy Spirit in Acts. A form of the verb *pimplemi* indicates a filling by the Spirit for an act of bearing witness. This sort of filling repeats at the Spirit's initiative. The adverb *pleres* indicates the abiding character trait, "full" of the Spirit, that marks a mature follower of Christ.

5. Since the Holy Spirit is the Person of the Godhead who enables us to receive and respond to the possibilities of the kingdom of God within us, it is a serious thing to grieve Him or to quench His activity in our spirits (Eph. 4:30; 1 Thess. 5:19). Spend a few moments evaluating whether you have attitudes or patterns of behavior that interfere with the Spirit's kingdom work in your life. Record your conclusions in the space below.

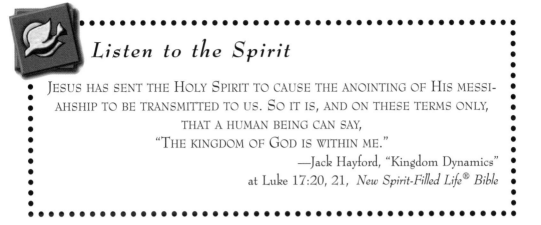

Listen to the Spirit

JESUS HAS SENT THE HOLY SPIRIT TO CAUSE THE ANOINTING OF HIS MESSI-
AHSHIP TO BE TRANSMITTED TO US. SO IT IS, AND ON THESE TERMS ONLY,
THAT A HUMAN BEING CAN SAY,
"THE KINGDOM OF GOD IS WITHIN ME."
—Jack Hayford, "Kingdom Dynamics"
at Luke 17:20, 21, *New Spirit-Filled Life® Bible*

6.   God the Father initiated the concept of the kingdom of God by creating the
      world and people. He provided a constitution by revealing His will and
      moral order in the Bible. God the Son was anointed King by His Father and
      claimed His throne by entering human experience through the Incarnation
      and redeeming His subjects by means of the Cross. The Holy Spirit acti-
      vates and energizes the Son's kingdom rule in His subjects' lives in the pres-
      ent age. It is, therefore, a spiritual kingdom until the Second Coming of the
      Lord Jesus at the end of the age. How do you want the kingdom of God to
      be expressed in each of the following areas of your life? What do you need
      to do to see your desires realized?

Your worship of God

Your witness for Christ

Your work in a career or at home

Your marriage or closest friendships

Your heritage you will leave at the end of life

7. In the space provided or on a separate sheet, write a pledge of allegiance to the kingdom of God and the King of kings who rules it. You may want to model it after the pledge of allegiance to the flag of the United States.

KINGDOM WARFARE

THERE IS OPEN hostility in the world between the kingdom of light and the kingdom of darkness, the forces of Christ and the forces of Satan, until the Lord returns and every knee bows to Him (Phil. 2:9–11). If you enthrone the Lord Jesus on your praises and submit every aspect of your life to His control as your King, you are at war with the forces of darkness. With the kingdom of God within you, you are subject to attack by the enemy, and you may be called on to strike against a work or stronghold of his.

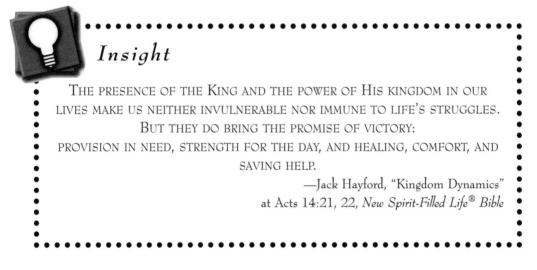

Insight

THE PRESENCE OF THE KING AND THE POWER OF HIS KINGDOM IN OUR LIVES MAKE US NEITHER INVULNERABLE NOR IMMUNE TO LIFE'S STRUGGLES. BUT THEY DO BRING THE PROMISE OF VICTORY: PROVISION IN NEED, STRENGTH FOR THE DAY, AND HEALING, COMFORT, AND SAVING HELP.

—Jack Hayford, "Kingdom Dynamics"
at Acts 14:21, 22, *New Spirit-Filled Life® Bible*

One of the most explicit passages in the New Testament about spiritual warfare in the kingdom of God is Ephesians 6:10–20. Strength is in the Lord (6:10). The weapons come from God (6:13). The opponent is a highly organized evil empire under the devil's command (6:11, 12). Paul is an "ambassador" (6:20) and all believers are armored soldiers of the Lord (6:11–17). Read Ephesians 6:10–20 and answer the following questions.

1. What does each of these elements in Ephesians 6:11, 12 suggest about the enemies of the kingdom of God?

The wiles of the devil

We do not wrestle against flesh and blood

But against principalities, against powers

Against the rulers of the darkness of this age

Against spiritual hosts of wickedness in the heavenly places

2.   In Ephesians 6:11–17, the armor of God consists of some matters of character (truth, righteousness, and faith) and some matters of learning (the gospel of peace, salvation, and the Word of God). What lies, accusations, temptations, or attacks of the devil can you see each of these pieces of armor protecting you from in spiritual warfare?

The belt of truth

The breastplate of righteousness

Footwear of the preparation of the gospel of peace

The shield of faith

The helmet of salvation

The sword of the Spirit (the Word of God)

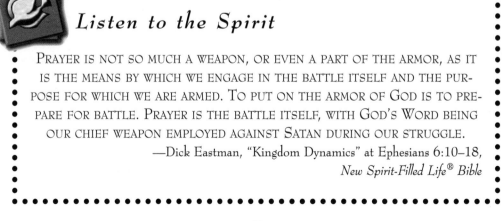

Listen to the Spirit

PRAYER IS NOT SO MUCH A WEAPON, OR EVEN A PART OF THE ARMOR, AS IT IS THE MEANS BY WHICH WE ENGAGE IN THE BATTLE ITSELF AND THE PURPOSE FOR WHICH WE ARE ARMED. TO PUT ON THE ARMOR OF GOD IS TO PREPARE FOR BATTLE. PRAYER IS THE BATTLE ITSELF, WITH GOD'S WORD BEING OUR CHIEF WEAPON EMPLOYED AGAINST SATAN DURING OUR STRUGGLE.
—Dick Eastman, "Kingdom Dynamics" at Ephesians 6:10–18, *New Spirit-Filled Life® Bible*

3. Paul viewed the armor of God as preparation for assault through prayer on the fortresses of the rulers of darkness in the heavenly places (Eph. 6:12, 18–20). What does each of these elements of verse 18 suggest about the seriousness of spiritual warfare through prayer?

Prayer and supplication in the Spirit

Watchful . . . with all perseverance

Supplication for all the saints

Intense spiritual warfare involving close contact with entrenched demonic forces is not for new recruits to the Lord's army, for the spiritually immature, or for those compromised as warriors by sin in their lives. Perhaps Satan's most successful strategy in spiritual warfare is to lull Christians into ignoring the New Testament's teaching about the clash between the kingdom of God and the realm of Satan. There are Christians whose spiritual gifts equip them uniquely to play major roles as spiritual warriors, but all of us are commanded to arm ourselves and pray.

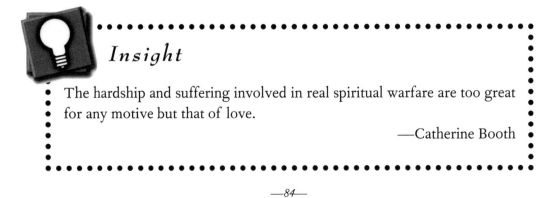

Insight

The hardship and suffering involved in real spiritual warfare are too great for any motive but that of love.

—Catherine Booth

5. Circle the letter of the statement below that best expresses your attitude toward the subject of spiritual warfare. In the space beneath the options, record your thoughts about how you need to adjust your attitude toward this serious activity (whether toward greater assertiveness or greater caution and humility).

   a. I'm not listening. I have my hands over my ears.

   b. This scares me, but I need to begin to work on my preparation for warfare.

   c. I am spiritually unfit because of sin in my life.

   d. I'm a new Christian and I don't know the Bible, how to pray, or much about any of this.

   e. I'm a growing Christian who needs to take spiritual warfare more seriously.

   f. I've participated on prayer teams in warfare against spiritual strongholds, and I wasn't ready for the intensity and the duration of the battle.

   g. My gifts, my temperament, and the maturity of my walk with the Lord make spiritual warfare an activity I engage in humbly but successfully.

   h. I love this sort of thing. Bring it on. I'm pumped.

6. Look back over the five studies in this chapter concerning "Spirit-Filled Kingdom Living." What are the three primary applications of truth that you want to implement in your life right away?

   1.

   2.

   3.

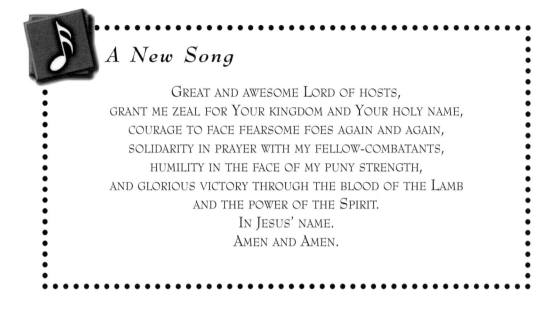

A New Song

GREAT AND AWESOME LORD OF HOSTS,
GRANT ME ZEAL FOR YOUR KINGDOM AND YOUR HOLY NAME,
COURAGE TO FACE FEARSOME FOES AGAIN AND AGAIN,
SOLIDARITY IN PRAYER WITH MY FELLOW-COMBATANTS,
HUMILITY IN THE FACE OF MY PUNY STRENGTH,
AND GLORIOUS VICTORY THROUGH THE BLOOD OF THE LAMB
AND THE POWER OF THE SPIRIT.
IN JESUS' NAME.
AMEN AND AMEN.

CHAPTER 4

SPIRIT-FILLED WISDOM

Our modern world is filled with intelligence. It's crawling with people we call "smart" and many cultures hold education in high regard. But let us not forget what cannot be learned from textbooks or purchased by tuition payments—the wisdom of God, which is imparted by His Spirit. In a nutshell, wisdom is nothing more than simply knowing exactly what the Lord would have you do in any situation. And the wisdom of God is not reserved for preachers or presidents or people who make decisions of global import. It is infinitely practical. Godly wisdom applies to everything from the way you conduct yourself in a business meeting to the way you manage your finances to the way you raise your children. Walking in wisdom will produce good fruit in your life and is crucial to abundant living. It will guide you into good decisions and sound judgment, which everyone needs in the twenty-first century! Are you ready to live wisely?

Insight

Wisdom is the power to see and the inclination to choose the best and highest goal, together with the surest means of attaining it.

—J. I. Packer, *Knowing God*

SEEKING WISDOM

BIBLICAL WISDOM IS not a function of intelligence. Wisdom is a spiritual quality that produces skillful, godly living. Wisdom is partly learned from the Bible and spiritual models and partly bestowed by the Holy Spirit in response to earnest prayer. The fact that wisdom must be learned indicates that time and effort has to be expended. In that sense, wisdom is related to maturity. The fact that wisdom must be given by the Spirit indicates that God can sovereignly and surprisingly increase the maturity level of an earnest seeker.

1. Read the following passages of Scripture and note what each says about how to seek wisdom.

Proverbs 1:8, 9

Proverbs 2:1–6

Proverbs 3:11–13

Proverbs 8:1–6

James 1:2–8

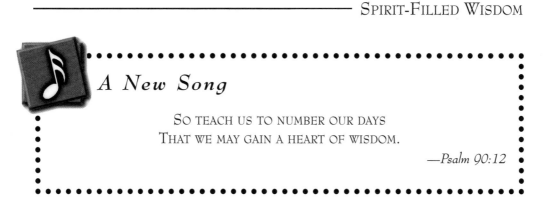

A New Song

SO TEACH US TO NUMBER OUR DAYS
THAT WE MAY GAIN A HEART OF WISDOM.

—*Psalm 90:12*

2. The wisdom of God for which we are to seek is not the philosophical speculation that the world often calls wisdom. Read the following passages and note how the apostle Paul distinguished the wisdom of God.

1 Corinthians 1:20–25—how the godly wisdom differs from worldly wisdom

1 Corinthians 1:26–31—how wisdom relates to Jesus

1 Corinthians 2:4–11—how wisdom relates to the Holy Spirit

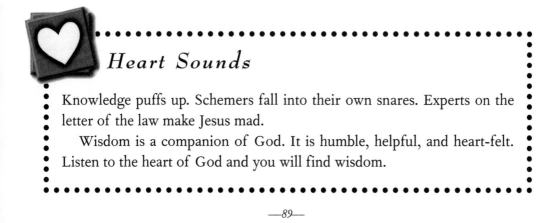

Heart Sounds

Knowledge puffs up. Schemers fall into their own snares. Experts on the letter of the law make Jesus mad.

Wisdom is a companion of God. It is humble, helpful, and heart-felt. Listen to the heart of God and you will find wisdom.

3.   The Book of Proverbs offers the hope and help of wisdom to four classes of spiritually needy people: the simple, the fool, the scoffer, and the sluggard. At times, we all find traits of each of these in our thinking and behavior. How can seeking wisdom rescue us when we act in these ways?

The Simple: a naïve or immature person who is easily swayed by worldly influences (Prov. 1:4; 9:4–6; 1 Cor. 1:28–31; James 3:13)

The Fool: a rebel who chooses his own way over the Lord's way (Prov. 3:11, 12; 26:4, 5 [where *according to his folly* is used with two very different meanings]; James 3:14–18)

The Scoffer: a cynic who delights in mocking the truth and those who follow it (Prov. 9:7–8; 19:29; 1 Cor. 1:23, 24; James 4:1–3)

The Sluggard: a lazy person who justifies procrastination (Prov. 6:6–11; James 1:6–8)

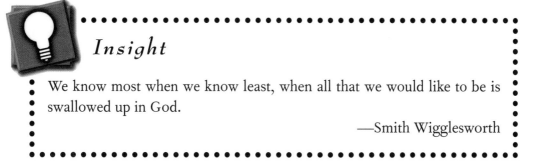

Insight

We know most when we know least, when all that we would like to be is swallowed up in God.

—Smith Wigglesworth

4. Following is a list of characteristics of godly wisdom. Put a plus sign (+) next to each of the statements that describes your level of wisdom. Put a minus sign (–) next to each of the statements that doesn't describe your level of wisdom.

a. God-fearing   h. Christ-centered

b. Peace-loving   i. Spirit-empowered

c. Prudent   j. Despised by the worldly proud

d. Discerning   k. Single-minded

e. Just   l. Gentle

f. Diligent   m. Reasonable

g. Humble

5. In what areas of your life do you currently feel in great need of supernatural wisdom? How can you go about asking, seeking, and knocking (Matt. 7:10) in order to find wisdom? (Remember, you need to work to learn wisdom as well as pray for it to be given.)

WISDOM AND THE FEAR OF GOD

THE FEAR OF God is a difficult topic to discuss. It's easier to say what it isn't than what it is. God doesn't want us to live in terror of Him. God doesn't want us chewing our fingernails with anxiety that He is going to hurt us because we sinned.

So what is the fear of the Lord, and what does it have to do with wisdom?

1.   How does the Bible relate wisdom and the fear of the Lord?

Positively (Ex. 20:20; Ps. 111:10; Prov. 1:7; 9:10; 15:33; Is. 33:6)

Negatively (Ps. 10:4; 14:1; Prov. 14:12; Jer. 5:20–25)

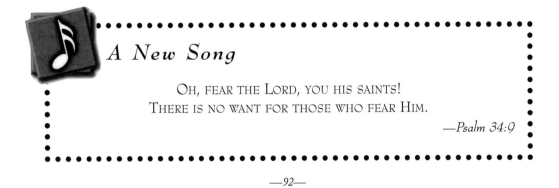

A New Song

OH, FEAR THE LORD, YOU HIS SAINTS!
THERE IS NO WANT FOR THOSE WHO FEAR HIM.

—Psalm 34:9

2. Job, in physical anguish caused by illness and emotional anguish caused by judgmental friends, questioned the justice of God (Job 27:2–6; 38:35–37). Instead of answering Job's questions, God revealed His glory to him (38—41). As a result:

What did Job conclude about himself (Job 40:3–5; 42:3, 6)?

What did Job conclude about God (Job 42:1, 2, 4–6)?

What did God think of Job's response to Him (Job 42:7–9)?

3. It's a mistake to think that God wants His worshipers to grovel in terror before Him. He wants us to catch sight of as much of His majesty and glory as we can bear. That will always be a frightening, awe-inspiring experience. Once we are appropriately shaken by His might and splendor, the Lord makes a uniform response to those who tremble before Him. In the following passages, note the person(s) involved, the fear-inducing situation, and the Lord's response.

Genesis 15:1

Exodus 20:20

Matthew 14:25–31

Luke 5:8–10

Revelation 1:17

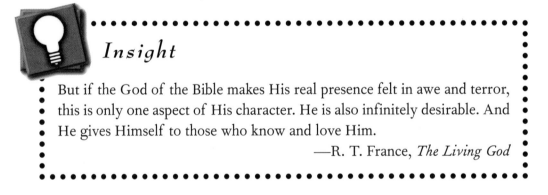

Insight

But if the God of the Bible makes His real presence felt in awe and terror, this is only one aspect of His character. He is also infinitely desirable. And He gives Himself to those who know and love Him.

—R. T. France, *The Living God*

4. As we saw in Chapter 2, "Spirit-Filled Worship," the fear of God is a doorway for praise and worship. Our God is an awesome God. In turn, praise and worship welcome the kingdom of God into our lives. When Christ reigns in our lives, we seek to do His will. The set of spiritual attitudes and skills necessary to carry out the will of God can be called "wisdom." They all begin with reverential fear. Read Luke 5:1–11 and record how you see each of the following operating in this story.

Fear of God

The Will of God

The Kingdom of God

Wisdom

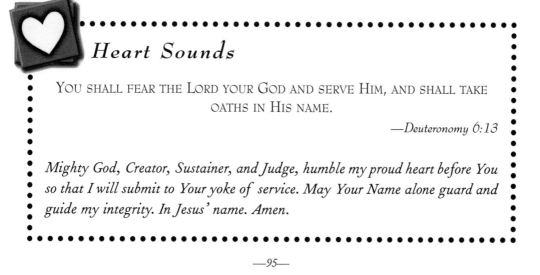

Heart Sounds

YOU SHALL FEAR THE LORD YOUR GOD AND SERVE HIM, AND SHALL TAKE OATHS IN HIS NAME.

—*Deuteronomy 6:13*

Mighty God, Creator, Sustainer, and Judge, humble my proud heart before You so that I will submit to Your yoke of service. May Your Name alone guard and guide my integrity. In Jesus' name. Amen.

5. Think back through your Christian life and recall times when you have been awed by the power and glory of God. Record the circumstances and what it was about God that moved you to reverent fear.

6. Circle the letter of the statement that best expresses how you think the fear of the Lord has produced wisdom in your life.

    a. I'm afraid of God's judgment so I stay away from sin.

    b. I am so amazed by God's might that I'm not afraid to try anything for Him.

    c. The awesome holiness of God inspires me to personal purity.

    d. The majesty of God's creation moves me to understand His ways.

    e. The splendor of God's absolute sovereignty prompts me to submit to His will.

    f. Other:

WISDOM AND SPEECH

PROBABLY NO BEHAVIOR is linked with wisdom more often in the Bible than speech. That shouldn't surprise us when we realize that God is a self-revealing God who values words as a primary means of revelation. We know the wisdom of God primarily through words He gave us in the Bible. We show our possession of wisdom or our lack of wisdom in large measure through our words. Jesus said, *"For out of the abundance of the heart the mouth speaks"* (Matt. 12:34). James brooded, *No man can tame the tongue. It is an unruly evil* (James 3:8). Solomon counseled, *The preparations of the heart belong to man, but the answer of the tongue is from the Lord* (Prov. 16:1). How can we prepare our hearts to receive wisdom from the Spirit of God to guide our speech?

1. Not surprisingly, the Book of Proverbs contains many epigrams about wise and foolish speech. Look up the following representative proverbs and note what each says about the power of speech.

   Proverbs 11:9

   Proverbs 12:18

   Proverbs 14:23

   Proverbs 15:1

Proverbs 16:24

Proverbs 16:27, 28

Proverbs 25:11, 12

2. The following proverbs contain positive and negative advice about how to speak. Summarize these wise sayings in the spaces provided.

Proverbs 10:19

Proverbs 11:13

Proverbs 12:17, 19

Proverbs 14:23

Proverbs 15:28

Proverbs 22:11

Proverbs 26:24–26

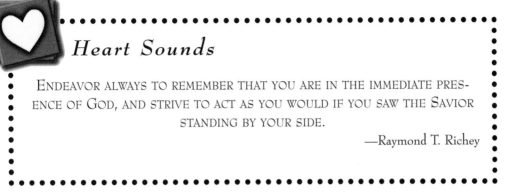

Heart Sounds

Endeavor always to remember that you are in the immediate presence of God, and strive to act as you would if you saw the Savior standing by your side.

—Raymond T. Richey

3. Circle the letter(s) of the statement(s) in the following list of unwise, harmful speech patterns that you identify as true of you.

   a. I vent my anger on people through cutting comments.

   b. I repeat stories about people that could harm them.

   c. I am sarcastic to the point of hurting others' feelings.

   d. I talk too much and think too little about what I say.

   e. I try to impress people by sounding well-informed.

   f. I like to argue.

   g. I tend to lie.

   h. I gripe and complain too much.

   i. I tend to tattle to people in authority about those around me.

   j. I am tactless and hurtfully blunt.

   k. I am ungrateful and seldom compliment people who do well.

   l. Other:

4. Circle the letter(s) of the statement(s) in the following list of wise, helpful speech patterns that you identify as true of you.

   a. I am generally encouraging of others in my speech.

   b. I tell the truth and avoid exaggeration.

   c. I thank others and praise their accomplishment.

    d.   I think before I speak.

    e.   I say the same thing to important and ordinary people.

    f.   I speak humbly about myself and my accomplishments.

    g.   I acknowledge to others the Lord's presence and activity in my life.

    h.   I am kind and gentle in my speech to others.

    i.   My humor is positive and uplifting.

    j.   I listen well in conversation.

    k.   People seek my advice.

    l.   Other:

5.   James is the New Testament writer who most reflects the Old Testament wisdom of Proverbs. Read James 3:2–12. What are the dangers James wrote about of a tongue controlled by "earthly, sensual, demonic" wisdom (3:15)?

6.   Read James 4:5–12. What is the message from the Spirit of God to all who want their speech controlled by *the wisdom that is from above* (James 3:17)?

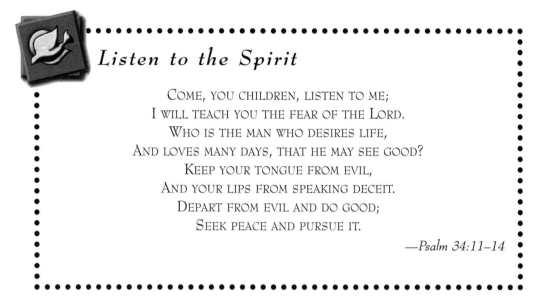

Listen to the Spirit

COME, YOU CHILDREN, LISTEN TO ME;
I WILL TEACH YOU THE FEAR OF THE LORD.
WHO IS THE MAN WHO DESIRES LIFE,
AND LOVES MANY DAYS, THAT HE MAY SEE GOOD?
KEEP YOUR TONGUE FROM EVIL,
AND YOUR LIPS FROM SPEAKING DECEIT.
DEPART FROM EVIL AND DO GOOD;
SEEK PEACE AND PURSUE IT.

—Psalm 34:11–14

7. Spend a few moments asking the Spirit of God to impress on you what you should do about one or more of the negative speech characteristics you marked in item 3. Write the response from Him that you sense.

8. Spend a few moments asking the Spirit of God which of the positive speech qualities from item 4 you should improve and how. Write the response from Him that you sense.

A New Song

C. S. Lewis observed, "It is in their 'good' characters that novelists make, unawares, the most shocking self-revelations" (*A Preface to Paradise Lost*). Stories abound with interesting bad characters and dull good ones. Why? Because we all, writers and readers, have so much more experience with evil than with good. The apostle Paul counseled the Roman believers, "I want you to be wise in what is good, and simple concerning evil" (Rom. 16:19). Make this especially true in your speech.

WISDOM AND DISCERNMENT

SOME CHRISTIANS HAVE the spiritual gift of discerning spirits (1 Cor. 12:10), but all of us need to develop the level of spiritual discernment we are capable of under the guidance of the Holy Spirit. Paul Walker's article on "Holy Spirit Gifts and Power" (*New Spirit-Filled Life® Bible*, p. 1857) refers to "spiritual insight," especially when it comes to recognizing the plans and purposes of Satan. Joe Stowell, President of Moody Bible Institute, asserts, "We must be prepared to distinguish light from darkness, truth from error, best from better, righteousness from unrighteousness, purity from defilement, and principles from pragmatics" (*Fan the Flame*).

Discernment of spirits may involve sensing demonic activity in a situation. It may also involve detecting an ignoble motive behind the criticism of one Christian by another.

1. Rate your spiritual discernment on the following scale by circling the number that indicates your perception of this ability.

1	2	3	4	5	6	7	8	9	10
Unaware		Often Confused		Generally Aware		Pretty Alert	Never		Miss

2. Circle the letter(s) of the statement(s) that best capture your attitude toward spiritual discernment.

   a. I don't want anything to do with demons!

   b. I don't like to be judgmental.

   c. This sounds serious. I would be very cautious about this.

   d. I've needed to work on this for a long time.

   e. I can't wait to tangle with dark forces!

   f. Other:

3. Are you satisfied with the attitude you expressed in item 2? Why or why not?

4. The fourth chapter of 1 John begins with a discussion of false prophets troubling the churches to which the apostle was writing. He acknowledged that a spirit prompted every religious teacher, but denied that it was always the Holy Spirit (4:2, 3). Read 1 John 4:1–6. How were John's readers to distinguish the spirit of the Antichrist/spirit of error from the Holy Spirit/spirit of truth?

Heart Sounds

If we have the Holy Ghost we can prove the spirits, because everything the Holy Ghost does is confirmed by the Word . . .everything must be measured by the Word.

—Maria Woodworth-Etter

5. In 1 John, discernment was based on a doctrinal criterion. What was the standard for discerning spirits in each of these cases?

Matthew 7:15–23

Mark 9:17–22

Acts 8:14–24

Acts 16:16–19

1 Corinthians 6:1–8

2 Peter 2:1–3, 10–14

Revelation 2:2–5

Grace Notes

I had occasion to travel to India in 1996. During that trip several of us visited a village near Madras. Eric Derry, our missions minister, Toni Wright, a prayer warrior on the trip with us, and I sat on a low cot in the middle of the village. As we prayed, a dog, which was standing next to Toni and which had been restlessly silent up till then, began to bark and yap its head off. I was a bit irritated but didn't think too much of the situation until Toni, in anger, suddenly stopped praying, turned toward the dog, and blurted, "In the name of Jesus, be silent!" The dog stopped instantly and went away as fast as it could with its tail between its legs.

—Rick Stacy, Meridian Christian Church

6. Imagine that a couple begins attending your church, and you strike up a friendship with them. They have moved to your town from Amsterdam, where the husband worked for an import-export business. After a while, you discover the wife is falling into depression. She is losing weight, sleeping badly, and experiencing violent, ghoulish dreams. In the course of conversation, you find she dabbled in occult practices before coming to faith in Christ a year ago. Circle the letter(s) of the following statement(s) that apply to what you would do to discern what is happening here.

   a. Refer her to your pastor and pray for her.

   b. Recommend a complete physical exam by her doctor.

   c. Consult with church leaders about what spiritual, emotional, and physical factors might be involved.

   d. Recommend the church elders anoint and pray for her.

   e. Fast and pray for wisdom to discern what is going on.

   f. Lay hands on her and command the demons to leave in the name of Jesus.

   g. Involve a team of intercessors to engage in spiritual warfare on her behalf.

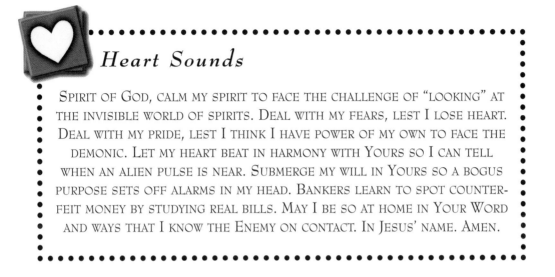

Heart Sounds

SPIRIT OF GOD, CALM MY SPIRIT TO FACE THE CHALLENGE OF "LOOKING" AT THE INVISIBLE WORLD OF SPIRITS. DEAL WITH MY FEARS, LEST I LOSE HEART. DEAL WITH MY PRIDE, LEST I THINK I HAVE POWER OF MY OWN TO FACE THE DEMONIC. LET MY HEART BEAT IN HARMONY WITH YOURS SO I CAN TELL WHEN AN ALIEN PULSE IS NEAR. SUBMERGE MY WILL IN YOURS SO A BOGUS PURPOSE SETS OFF ALARMS IN MY HEAD. BANKERS LEARN TO SPOT COUNTER-FEIT MONEY BY STUDYING REAL BILLS. MAY I BE SO AT HOME IN YOUR WORD AND WAYS THAT I KNOW THE ENEMY ON CONTACT. IN JESUS' NAME. AMEN.

WISDOM AND RADICAL DISCIPLESHIP

THE WISDOM OF Proverbs is the wisdom of many counselors, long experience, and obedience to the righteous demands of God's Law. Does wisdom have anything to do with obeying God's Spirit when He prompts us to take outrageous risks? For instance, is it wise to leave one's family and home to serve as a career missionary in an unstable third-world country?

Sometimes it seems there are two kinds of faith in Christian living. There is steady faith in the truth of God's Word that leads us into lives of morality and integrity. We become solid citizens, productive employees, dependable church members, loyal friends, loving spouses, caring parents, and faithful followers of Jesus. Then God asks us to do something risky for the kingdom, or He permits tragedy to rock our lives. Suddenly there is need for mountain-moving faith. What's the relationship between faith for routine living and faith for crisis living? What's the relationship between wisdom for routine living and wisdom for crisis living?

A New Song

SOVEREIGN LORD, GIVE ME EARS TO HEAR AND EYES TO SEE THAT I MAY NOT MISTAKE YOUR VOICE OR MISS THE SIGNPOSTS ALONG THE PATH. TRAIN ME IN THE USUAL THINGS, THAT I MAY BE READY FOR THE UNUSUAL ONES. GIVE ME HUMILITY AND PATIENCE, SO THAT I MAY HAVE COURAGE AND DECISIVENESS. LET ME KNOW YOUR SPIRIT SO WELL IN PEACEFUL TIMES THAT I WILL NOT MISTAKE HIM IN TIMES OF CRISIS. IN JESUS' NAME. AMEN.

1. Sometimes we think there are superstar Christians who are always having spectacular spiritual experiences and ordinary Christians who lead uneventful spiritual lives. Everybody lives ordinary lives sprinkled with opportunities for extraordinary spiritual experiences. Some Christians respond to them and see God do remarkable things through them. Others don't. Read the following Scriptures and write what each says about the relationship between the ordinary and the extraordinary.

Matthew 7:24–27

Matthew 25:14–30

Luke 16:10–13

James 1:2–8

1 Peter 5:5–11

2. In what areas of your life do you think God expects you to demonstrate consistent faithfulness before His Spirit will entrust you with greater spiritual responsibility? List them below. After each, indicate how you would rate your faithfulness in each of these areas?

3. Faithfulness, obedience, and humility during the ordinary seasons of our spiritual lives produce the character needed for faithfulness, obedience, and humility in the extraordinary moments of our spiritual lives. How did each of these biblical characters recognize the voice of God calling them to radical discipleship in one of those extraordinary moments?

Acts 10:9–23

Acts 11:19–26

Acts 13:6–12

Acts 16:16–18

Acts 16:25–34

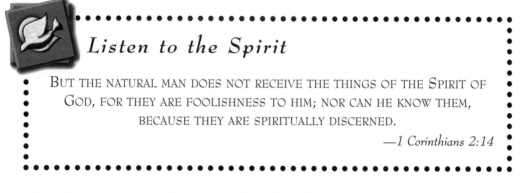

Listen to the Spirit

BUT THE NATURAL MAN DOES NOT RECEIVE THE THINGS OF THE SPIRIT OF GOD, FOR THEY ARE FOOLISHNESS TO HIM; NOR CAN HE KNOW THEM, BECAUSE THEY ARE SPIRITUALLY DISCERNED.

—1 Corinthians 2:14

4. How have you at times sensed God's Spirit prompting you to speak or act for Him? How did you respond to these situations? What were the outcomes?

5. The natural human tendency when faced with promptings of the Holy Spirit toward an unusual form of obedience is to procrastinate and look for some "explanation" that softens the call to radical discipleship. What do these Scriptures suggest are the dangers of ignoring or minimizing the Spirit's unusual challenges?

Luke 19:20–26

Ephesians 4:30

1 Thessalonians 5:19

6. What (if any) unusual challenge(s) have you been sensing from God recently? How can you test this spirit, and how should you respond if you believe this is the Holy Spirit speaking to you? Be specific.

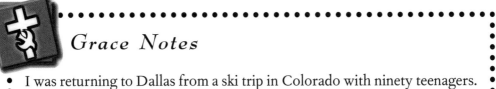

Grace Notes

I was returning to Dallas from a ski trip in Colorado with ninety teenagers. A blizzard struck and we were snowbound Christmas Eve 1973 in Trinidad, Colorado. The weather broke Christmas morning, but one iced-up diesel engine would not start. I gathered some kids who had come to faith on that trip, and we prayed the bus would start. Then I felt compelled to tell the driver, in the presence of the teens, that we had prayed and the bus was going to start. It started on the next attempt. The high schoolers were strengthened in their new faith, and the driver was still talking about the incident the next week when he drove another Young Life ski trip.

—Joe Snider

CHAPTER 5

SPIRIT-FILLED VICTORY OVER SIN

The Spirit-filled life is a victorious life, but that does not mean it is free from temptation or challenge. In order to grow strong and to develop spiritual "muscle", we have to have something to push against, something to withstand. This opposition often presents itself in the form of temptation to sin and, according to Romans 6:16, sin leads to death. Our goal is to be kingdom people on the journey of abundant life, growing in strength and overcoming the obstacles before us.* Are you ready to learn how to gain victory over sin?

DAY 1 — DEAD TO SIN

THE BIBLE'S TEACHING about sin and the Christian falls into two big categories: what happened when Jesus died on the Cross and what happens in the daily life of a Christian? On the Cross, Jesus paid the penalty for sin, obtained forgiveness for sin, and defeated sin and Satan. In daily life, forgiven Christians wrestle with the residual effects of their sinful nature and the temptations of the world, the flesh, and the devil. Often we find ourselves asking: if sin and Satan were

---

* Jesus our King was tempted, but remained sinless. As we serve Him and follow Him, let us seek to resist temptation as well.

defeated decisively on the Cross, why do they seem to exert so much influence in the lives of believers?

1. Circle the number of the following statement that best describes your experience of victory over sin in your life.

    a. I surrender my life daily to Christ and experience consistent victory over sin.

    b. I confess my sins regularly and enjoy uninterrupted fellowship with God.

    c. Sometimes I am careless about admitting and dealing with my sins; sometimes I confess them and ask forgiveness.

    d. I think about my sins when I am in church and I am sorry for them and feel better.

    e. My life is dominated by one or more sins I cannot get victory over.

    f. Other:

2. What insight, motivation, or behavioral change would you like to achieve through this five day consideration of victory over sin?

In order to approach the topic of victory over sin, it's important to begin with what the Bible says about the death of Jesus in relation to Christians and sin. There are many passages that address this topic. Let's look at two in Romans and identify some key theological ideas.

3. Read Romans 5:8–10 and describe the past, present, and future benefits noted in this text that we enjoy through the sacrificial death of Jesus for our sins.

Past

Present

Future

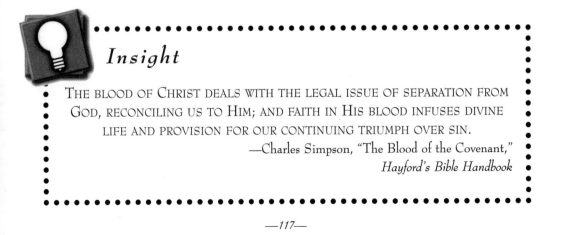

Insight

THE BLOOD OF CHRIST DEALS WITH THE LEGAL ISSUE OF SEPARATION FROM GOD, RECONCILING US TO HIM; AND FAITH IN HIS BLOOD INFUSES DIVINE LIFE AND PROVISION FOR OUR CONTINUING TRIUMPH OVER SIN.
—Charles Simpson, "The Blood of the Covenant,"
Hayford's Bible Handbook

4. Romans 6—8 is Paul's premier passage dealing with the Christian's daily experience with sin. Read Romans 6:1–14 and record your observations and thoughts about this Scripture in response to the following questions.

What should be our basic daily attitude toward sin?

On what basis can we maintain that this is an appropriate attitude?

What should our basic attitude be toward the life we lead every day?

On what basis can we maintain that this is an appropriate attitude?

What should be your battle plan for approaching any temptations to sin that a day might hold for you?

Heart Sounds

A murmuring spirit is often the cause of lack of victory. When the children of Israel murmured, they grieved and angered God. We are commanded to "offer the sacrifice of praise to God continually"—not merely with our hearts but with our lips. And if we obey this command there will not be much room left for murmuring.

—Carrie Judd Montgomery

5. Compare Romans 6:13 with the more familiar Romans 12:1, 2. It takes a radical renewal of our thinking and consciousness to live with the moment-by-moment awareness that we are dead to sin and alive to righteousness. It takes great determination to live that spiritual truth in the power of the Holy Spirit. Read Romans 8:2–4, 9–11. Meditate on those verses and the following questions. Record the results of your communion with God's Spirit in the space below.

How does God's Spirit energize me to defeat temptation and sin and to live a holy life?

What do I need to do (or stop doing) to give the Holy Spirit this kind of control of my life?

Listen to the Spirit

For the good that I will to do, I do not do; but the evil I will not to do, that I practice. . . . O wretched man that I am! Who will deliver me from this body of death?

But if the Spirit of Him who raised Jesus from the dead dwells in you, He who raised Christ from the dead will also give life to your mortal bodies through His Spirit who dwells in you.

I say then: Walk in the Spirit, and you shall not fulfill the lust of the flesh. For the flesh lusts against the Spirit, and the Spirit against the flesh; and these are contrary to one another, so that you do not do the things you wish."

—*Romans 7:19, 24; 8:11; Galatians 5:16, 17*

6. Below are some promises you could make to God in response to the truth that you are dead to sin but alive to righteousness through the power of the Spirit of God. Consider them carefully and then circle the letter of the promise that best expresses the response you are making.

   a. Every morning I will say aloud, "In Christ, I am dead to sin and alive to righteousness."

   b. I will give You the members of my body every day and specify the ones that lead me into sin.

   c. I will pray daily, "Holy Spirit, live the life of Jesus through me today."

   d. Father, I will live today aware that I am dead to the sin of

      _____.

   e. I will partner with _____ in mutual encouragement to die to sin and live to righteousness today.

   f. Other:

REGULAR CONFESSION AND REPENTENCE

CONFESSION AND REPENTANCE play their roles in conversion. Every sinner who comes to Christ for forgiveness must admit his sin (confession) and turn away from it to live a renewed life (repentance). Confession and repentance play their roles in the lives of born-again believers in Jesus. They play a maintenance role in dealing with the sinful failures of our lives. The world is a dirty place, and we need its effects washed away. Confession and repentance also play a sanctifying role in dealing with previously unrecognized aspects of sin in our lives. We have inherited a sin nature. As God's Spirit sharpens our spiritual eyesight, we discover traces of wickedness in our hearts that we had been unable to see before. We have to deal with that newly recognized sin.

1.   When God asked Adam in the Garden of Eden if he had eaten of the forbidden fruit, Adam said, *"The woman whom You gave to be with me, she gave me of the tree, and I ate"* (Gen. 3:12). Even though Adam admitted he ate the fruit, what was wrong with his "confession"?

2.   What do each of the following Scriptures tell us about the nature of genuine confession?

Leviticus 16:21

Joshua 7:19–21

Psalm 32:3–5

Matthew 5:23, 24

James 5:16

1 John 1:9

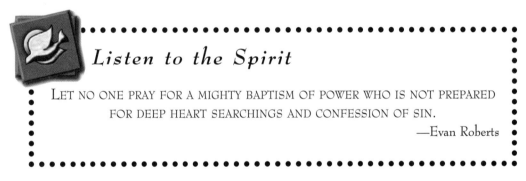

Listen to the Spirit

LET NO ONE PRAY FOR A MIGHTY BAPTISM OF POWER WHO IS NOT PREPARED
FOR DEEP HEART SEARCHINGS AND CONFESSION OF SIN.

—Evan Roberts

3. Repentance involves a new understanding that rejects a former course of action as wrong and embraces a new course of action that is right. Look at how Simon the sorcerer reacted to Peter's call for repentance in Acts 8:18–24. What was inadequate in his repentance?

4. What do the following Scriptures tell us regardimg the nature of genuine repentance?

1 Kings 8:46–51

Luke 3:8–14

2 Corinthians 7:9–11

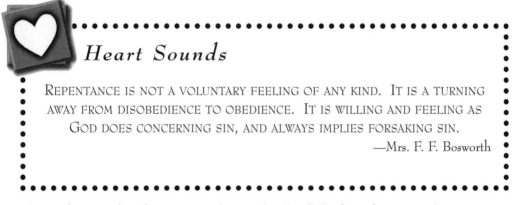

Heart Sounds

REPENTANCE IS NOT A VOLUNTARY FEELING OF ANY KIND. IT IS A TURNING AWAY FROM DISOBEDIENCE TO OBEDIENCE. IT IS WILLING AND FEELING AS GOD DOES CONCERNING SIN, AND ALWAYS IMPLIES FORSAKING SIN.
—Mrs. F. F. Bosworth

5. The apostle John compared a regular "walk" of confession and repentance to living in the beam of a searchlight that reveals the dirt in our lives. As each layer of grime is cleaned away, another shows underneath. It takes commitment to ultimate purity to stay in the light and let cleansing continue. Read 1 John 1:5–10 and answer the following questions based on that passage.

How does a Christian stay in the light and out of the dark?

The verbs *walk* and *cleanses* (1:7) are present tense and mean *keep on walking* and *keeps on cleansing*. What does the progressive nature of these verbs add to the ideas of confession and repentance in this passage?

Why does John say it's dangerous to deny the reality of sin when it is present in our lives?

6. Circle the letters of all of the statements in the following list that describe your present practice of confession and repentance.

   a. I make blanket statements, such as, "Forgive all the sins I committed today."

   b. I have premeditated sinful acts with the intention of "confessing" and "repenting" of them.

   c. I have habitual sins that it seems hypocritical to confess and repent because I do them so much.

   d. I confess and repent of my sins on a regular, systematic basis.

   e. I confess my sins to an accountability partner as part of my repentance to God.

   f. I repent publicly of my sins during invitations at church services.

   g. My confession includes naming my sins, and my repentance includes planning righteous behavior to replace the sins I am rejecting.

   h. My confession and repentance are most meaningful when I contrast the darkness of my sin with the bright light of God's holiness.

   i. Other:

7. Identify an area of your character or behavior that is "dark" in comparison to the light of God's holiness. Meditate on the holy character of God. From that meditation, write a prayer of confession and repentance.

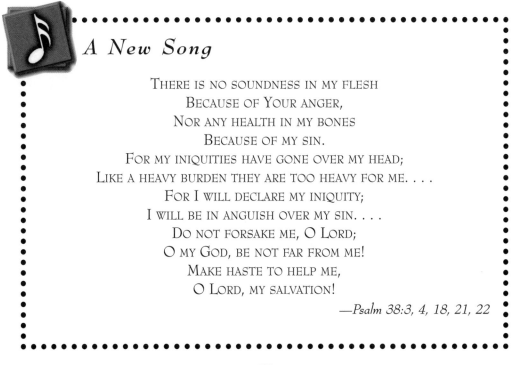

A New Song

There is no soundness in my flesh
Because of Your anger,
Nor any health in my bones
Because of my sin.
For my iniquities have gone over my head;
Like a heavy burden they are too heavy for me. . . .
For I will declare my iniquity;
I will be in anguish over my sin. . . .
Do not forsake me, O Lord;
O my God, be not far from me!
Make haste to help me,
O Lord, my salvation!

—*Psalm 38:3, 4, 18, 21, 22*

RESIST THE DEVIL

JESUS TAUGHT HIS disciples to pray, *And do not lead us into temptation, but deliver us from the evil one* (Matt. 6:13a). That line from the Lord's Prayer acknowledges that the path of our lives can pass through the vicinity of temptation and that the devil involves himself in trying to get us to sin. Jesus wants us to pray regularly that our heavenly Father will steer us clear of temptation and intervene on our behalf in any encounter with a snare of the devil.

1. Satan is the English form of a Hebrew word that means *the accuser*. An ordinary *satan* functioned as a prosecuting attorney. The Satan, the fallen archangel Lucifer, became the supreme spiritual accuser of people to God, to one another, and to themselves. The title "the devil" translates the Greek noun *diabolos*, which means *the slanderer*. The accusations of Satan may be true; the slanders of the devil are not. He is a liar from the beginning and the father of lies. In actuality, the evil one wraps his fact-based accusations in lying slanders to make them particularly poisonous to our spirits. Paul said, *We are not ignorant of his devices* (2 Cor. 2:11) and we must *stand against the wiles of the devil* (Eph. 6:11). Read the following Bible passages and summarize what each says about a different strategy of Satan.

2 Corinthians 11:14

Ephesians 4:26, 27

2 Thessalonians 2:9, 10

2 Timothy 2:26

Hebrews 2:14, 15

Revelation 12:10

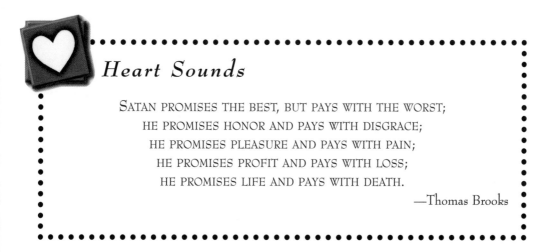

Heart Sounds

SATAN PROMISES THE BEST, BUT PAYS WITH THE WORST;
HE PROMISES HONOR AND PAYS WITH DISGRACE;
HE PROMISES PLEASURE AND PAYS WITH PAIN;
HE PROMISES PROFIT AND PAYS WITH LOSS;
HE PROMISES LIFE AND PAYS WITH DEATH.

—Thomas Brooks

The consistent perspective of the New Testament is that believers in Jesus must be prepared to resist the devil. There also is a consistent expectation that the devil will flee when he encounters a Christian who faces him in the power of the Lord. Jesus assumed His followers could encounter the devil with God's help

(Matt. 6:13; Luke 22:31). Paul wrote about resisting the devil (Eph. 4:27; 6:11). James and Peter also commanded their readers to resist the devil and gave instruction about how to prepare to face the archenemy.

2.   Read James 4:7–10. Answer the following questions based on this passage.

How do *drawing near to God* and *resisting the devil* relate to one another?

Why are clean hands and hearts necessary for approaching God and resisting the devil?

How do we purify our hands and hearts?

3.   Read 1 Peter 5:6–9, and answer these questions from this passage.

What positive spiritual attitudes are necessary for resisting the devil?

What negative spiritual attitudes will hinder resistance of the devil?

What attitudes toward suffering are necessary in order to resist the devil?

What role does humility play in resisting the devil in both James and 1 Peter?

Listen to the Spirit

Silence the attempts of the prince of darkness to intimidate God's children. His accusing voice of condemnation and guilt is swallowed up in the triumph of Calvary. Declare your abiding faith in the accomplished work of the Cross, and constantly participate in Jesus' ultimate victory, overcoming Satan by the power of the Cross and the steadfastness of your confession of faith in Christ's triumph.

—Roy Hicks, Sr., "Kingdom Dynamics" at Revelation 12:11,
New Spirit-Filled Life® Bible

4. Below is a list of possible strategies for resisting the devil. Circle the letters of the statements that describe tactics you have employed in the past. Put a star in front of the statements that describe tactics you want to employ in the future.

   a. I maintain an intimate, growing relationship with the Lord Jesus as my first line of defense against Satan.

   b. I counsel with spiritual leaders in my church about how to combat the devil.

   c. I regularly ask the Lord to keep me from temptation and deliver me from Satan.

   d. I fast and pray for extended periods when I feel assailed by the devil.

e. I enlist the prayer support of my small group or my friends when I sense opposition from the devil.

f. I ask my accountability partner to stand with me in resisting the devil.

g. I plead the blood of Christ for cleansing from sin and for protection from Satan.

h. I consciously humble myself before God so that His strength may lift me up in victory over the devil.

i. I use my God-given authority as His child to rebuke the devil and order him to flee.

j. I am careful not to speak carelessly and pridefully against Satan as though I were personally powerful.

k. Other:

5. On the following scale of 1 to 10, how would you rate your success in resisting the devil as he tries to deceive, defame, and destroy you?

1	2	3	4	5	6	7	8	9	10
Devoured		Bruised		PuttingUp A Fight		Winning More & More		Watching Him Run	

6. If you could ask an expert for practical help in resisting the devil, what would you want to know? In the space below, write your question(s) as you would like to ask it (them). After you record your questions, spend a moment asking God to lead you to someone who can help you.

A New Song

Mighty Father, strong to save, be Thou my buckler and shield on the day of fierce assault by the foe of all that is holy and true. I have done wrong; make my hands clean so I can stand in Thy presence. Make the words of my mouth and the meditations of my heart acceptable in Thy sight, O Lord, my Rock and my Redeemer. I kneel before Thee and wait for You to lift me up. That is the only way I want to stand. Indeed it is the only way I can stand against the evil one. Thank You for the powerful blood and name of Jesus. In Jesus' name. Amen.

BREAKING STRONGHOLDS

MANY PEOPLE FIND themselves struggling to conquer a habitual sin—a habit of the mind, a habit of the heart, or a habit of the flesh—that defies ordinary efforts to break it. Such habitual sin becomes a stumbling block to spiritual growth, the basis for regular condemnation by the devil, and a beachhead from which he can destroy a person's character, reputation, or life. Among these strongholds are addictive behaviors, obsessive thought processes, sins that function as regular coping mechanisms, and occult practices. Any repetitive physical, mental, or spiritual sin that becomes entrenched in our lives is a stronghold from which Satan can operate to frustrate the sanctifying purposes of the Holy Spirit and inject destruction into our lives.

1.   Ideally there are no spiritual strongholds in your life that need to be overthrown by God's power and Spirit. You may, even in that case, be susceptible in some area of life to a habitual sin. In the following list, circle the letter of any of these habitual sins that are major avenues of the devil's influence in your life. Put a star in front of the habitual sins that have become strongholds or that you fear are growing strong in your life.

a.	alcoholism	l.	stealing
b.	lying	m.	pyromania
c.	adultery	n.	gambling
d.	drug addiction	o.	clothing/physical appearance
e.	homosexual behavior	p.	nicotine in tobacco products
f.	eating disorder	q.	nursing grudges
g.	shopping	r.	fascination with death
h.	anger	s.	obsessive fantasizing
i.	pornography	t.	violence
j.	occultism	u.	addiction to television or electronic media
k.	masturbation	v.	Other:

2. Which of the following solutions describe ways you have tried in the past to deal with habitual behaviors you wanted to halt? Circle the letters of all statements that apply to you.

    a.   I ignore it and hope it will go away.

    b.   I exercise my will power.

    c.   I pray for God's assistance in stopping.

    d.   I use self-help devices or ideas.

    e.   I read books, listen to tapes, attend seminars.

    f.   I join a support group for help.

    g.   I counsel with my pastor or other spiritual leaders.

    h.   I depend on an accountability partner to help me.

    i.   I ask for prayer from several sources.

    j.   I ask the elders of my church to anoint me with oil and pray for deliverance.

    k.   I seek the help of an exorcist.

    l.   I visit a professional therapist.

    m.   I enter a treatment facility.

    n.   Other:

Insight

Fasting is repeatedly referred to throughout Scripture as a sacrificial form of prayer warfare that produces results available in no other way. . . . Fasting involves a sacrificial denying of necessary nourishment while turning one's attention to seeking God during that denial.

—Dick Eastman, "Kingdom Dynamics" at Ezra 8:21–23,
New Spirit-Filled Life® Bible

3. If you currently battle a life-dominating sin (or have in the past), describe below how this battle affects (or affected) your walk with the Lord and your outlook on life.

4. In previous explorations of passages such as Ephesians 6:10–20, James 4:7–10, and 1 Peter 5:6–9, you observed that our struggle with sin is part of the conflict between the powers of darkness and the powers of light— between the temporal realm of Satan and the eternal kingdom of God. Strongholds of evil in our lives need to be battled and conquered in the name of the Lord Jesus. Read 2 Corinthians 10:3–6 where the apostle Paul describes assault of spiritual strongholds. What does he say about these aspects of dealing with strongholds?

The weaponry

The nature of strongholds

The goal of the battle

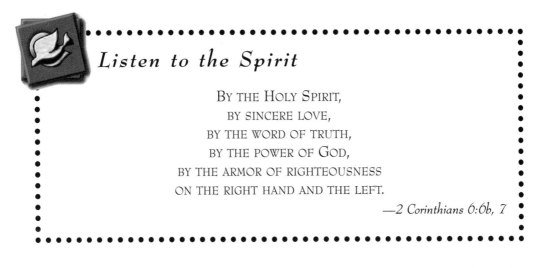

Listen to the Spirit

By the Holy Spirit,
by sincere love,
by the word of truth,
by the power of God,
by the armor of righteousness
on the right hand and the left.

—2 Corinthians 6:6b, 7

5. Look up the following passages and record what you discover about the spiritual weapons available to you.

Matthew 17:18–21

Mark 16:17, 18

Ephesians 6:17, 18

James 4:9, 10

6. Christians struggling against a spiritual stronghold need the power of the Holy Spirit and the assistance of others. Humility must precede exaltation (1 Pet. 5:6). The admission of need for help seems to be an integral part of the humility needed to gain victory over a spiritual stronghold. Look at the following Scriptures and record what each says about a "team" approach to conquering strongholds.

Matthew 18:18–20

Galatians 6:1, 2

James 5:13–16

7. If you identified an actual or potential spiritual stronghold in your life in item 3, reflect on how the Lord would have you begin to deal with it. Write your action plan below. Include others or your chances of victory are slight. If you did not identify a stronghold in item 3, reflect on how you might come alongside others and help them demolish their strongholds.

A New Song

Lord of hosts, set me free from irrational, compulsive sin. I am out of control and only Your Spirit can tame mine. Give me courage to admit my sin to others who can help me face my foe. Free me from shame, from despair, and from focus on myself. Let me love and serve You and others without distraction. Make my weakness a display case for Your strength. In Jesus' name. Amen.

DEMONIZATION

SOME PEOPLE SEE demons behind every sinful act, so that human responsibility almost disappears. Others see natural causes behind the most bizarre evil behaviors, so that evil spirits virtually disappear. The truth is that demons are both real and active. We may, on occasion, encounter their influence in and around the lives of unbelievers or believers.

Theologians have long debated whether a Christian can be demon possessed. In recent years, many Bible students have noted that the Greek verb *demonizo* is a term of affliction rather than possession. They coined the term *demonized* to express the influence of one or more demons in the life of an individual believer or unbeliever. While theologians theorize about the exact nature or extent of demonic affliction of children of God, we share our everyday world with a host of invisible angels and demons. They influence our lives for good and ill in ways we seldom perceive. If we do encounter a demonic presence, what would it look like? What should we do?

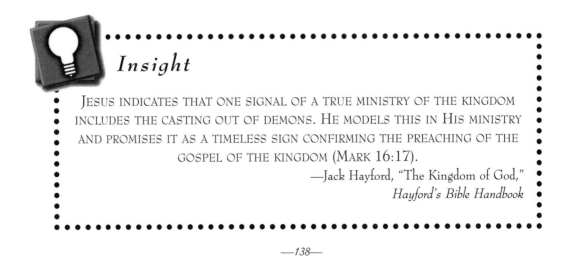

Insight

JESUS INDICATES THAT ONE SIGNAL OF A TRUE MINISTRY OF THE KINGDOM INCLUDES THE CASTING OUT OF DEMONS. HE MODELS THIS IN HIS MINISTRY AND PROMISES IT AS A TIMELESS SIGN CONFIRMING THE PREACHING OF THE GOSPEL OF THE KINGDOM (MARK 16:17).

—Jack Hayford, "The Kingdom of God,"
Hayford's Bible Handbook

1. A tremendous amount of discernment is needed to differentiate demonized behavior from the affects of mental or physical disorders. Read the following passages and list the behaviors caused by demons.

Judges 9:23, 24

1 Samuel 16:14–16, 23; 18:10, 11

Matthew 8:28; Acts 19:16

Mark 1:23, 24; John 10:20

Mark 1:26; Luke 9:37–42

2. Read the following passages and notice how the early Christians approached breaking the influence of demons over people.

Luke 10:17; Acts 16:18

Mark 9:28, 29

Ephesians 6:12, 18; Colossians 2:15

3.   On the following scale of 1 to 10, how would you rate your attitude toward
     the thought of encountering demonization?

1	2	3	4	5	6	7	8	9	10
Scared		Uncomfortable			Willing		Cautiously		Ready
Speechless					To Pray		Bold		To Confront

Heart Sounds

THE POWER OF GOD IS EQUAL TO EVERY EMERGENCY AND IS GREAT ENOUGH
FOR THE DELIVERANCE OF EVERY SOUL FROM EVERY OPPRESSION.
—John G. Lake

If you encounter bizarre behavior, a history of occult practice, or a resistant
spiritual stronghold that causes you to suspect demonic influence in someone's
life, seek the counsel of mature spiritual leaders. A power encounter with spirits
is not a game. It should be undertaken by a spiritually fit team of believers pro-
tected by a cover of prayer by intercessors.

4.   Occasionally you will hear someone attribute an act of sin or a sinful atti-
     tude to a demon—a specific spirit of lying or spirit of envy, for instance.

Which of these statements best expresses your opinion about attributing individual acts and attitudes to specific demons? Circle the letter of the statement.

  a. It relieves the sinner of his or her responsibility by implying, "The devil made me do it."

  b. Good and bad spirits probably influence our behaviors and attitudes, but they don't control our wills. We decide what to do.

  c. I think there are occasional acts and thoughts so bad and out of character for the person involved that demons may have caused them.

  d. Demons are always planting evil ideas in our heads. If our guard is down, they make us do bad things.

  e. Other:

5. Support your opinion about demonization and personal responsibility from item 4. Consider using biblical evidence, reasoning, and examples in your response.

Grace Notes

AND THOUGH THIS WORLD WITH DEVILS FILLED,
SHOULD THREATEN TO UNDO US,
WE WILL NOT FEAR, FOR GOD HATH WILLED
HIS TRUTH TO TRIUMPH THROUGH US.
THE PRINCE OF DARKNESS GRIM,
WE TREMBLE NOT FOR HIM—
HIS RAGE WE CAN ENDURE,
FOR LO, HIS DOOM IS SURE:
ONE LITTLE WORD SHALL FELL HIM.

THAT WORD ABOVE ALL EARTHLY POWERS,
NO THANKS TO THEM ABIDETH;
THE SPIRIT AND THE GIFTS ARE OURS
THROUGH HIM WHO WITH US SIDETH.
LET GOODS AND KINDRED GO,
THIS MORTAL LIFE ALSO—
HIS KINGDOM IS FOREVER.

—Martin Luther, "A Mighty Fortress Is Our God"

SPIRIT-FILLED RELATIONSHIPS

God's kingdom is full of relationships—relationships between believers and the Lord, and relationships between believers and other believers. In addition, most of our lives also include relationships with non-believers. In Peter's first letter to Christians in Asia Minor, he gives this directive, which is as relevant today as it was when he wrote it: "And above all things have fervent love for one another, for 'love will cover a multitude of sins.'" This is the key to kingdom relationships—fervent love for one another. Love is not always fun and love is not always easy, but love is always right and it is always obedient to the Lord's command. The Holy Spirit empowers us to have fervent love and love brings change to even difficult relationships. Are you ready to let the power of love impact your relationships?

FORGIVENESS

FORGIVENESS STANDS AT the heart of uniquely Christian relationships. Jesus made perhaps His most radical statement when He commanded us to, "Love your enemies." We can't love our enemies until we have forgiven them. The old saying, "To err is human, to forgive divine" acknowledges that we are acting like

God when we forgive, and although we may find forgiveness difficult, it is essential to a vibrant, Spirit-filled life.

1. Jesus taught the Lord's Prayer to His disciples—those who already had a saving relationship with Him. The forgiveness issues in the prayer are not a basis for salvation from the eternal punishment for sin. They are a basis for the quality of our relationships with God and other people. How does what goes on in our human relationships affect our relationship with God (Matt. 6:12, 14–15)?

Positively

Negatively

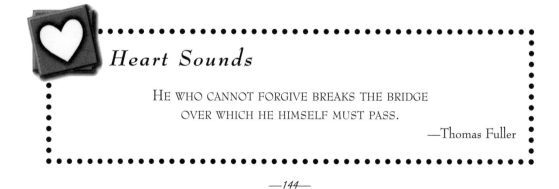

Heart Sounds

HE WHO CANNOT FORGIVE BREAKS THE BRIDGE
OVER WHICH HE HIMSELF MUST PASS.

—Thomas Fuller

2. Jesus devoted one of His strongest parables to underlining the spiritual necessity that those who have received God's forgiveness must forgive those who offend them. The occasion of the parable was Peter's question, *"Lord, how often shall my brother sin against me, and I forgive him? Up to seven times?"* (Matt. 18:21). Peter was looking for the limits of forgiveness beyond which he could take offense and seek revenge.

In Jesus' eyes, what are the limits of forgiveness (Matt. 18:22)?

Read the parable of the unforgiving servant in Matthew 18:23–35. What did it mean to the servant to be forgiven a great debt?

What is so outrageous about the forgiven servant refusing to forgive his fellow-servant?

Suppose the first servant said, "The master is rich. He can afford to forgive my huge debt. I'm poor. I cannot afford to forgive that small debt." Would you be swayed by that argument? Why or why not?

A parable is a story with one main point. It's not an allegory in which every detail of the story lines up with a parallel detail in our lives. The master in the story forgave his servant and then withdrew the forgiveness so he could punish him. The parable does not teach that God acts like that. The point is that when I try to protect myself by means of unforgiveness, I destroy myself instead. How does unforgiveness leave us in a state of emotional and spiritual torture?

Heart Sounds

THE HUMAN CAPACITY TO FORGET GOD'S GRACIOUS GIFT OF FORGIVENESS AND ALLOW SMALLNESS OF SOUL TO BREED UNFORGIVENESS IS SOBERINGLY WARNED AGAINST. . . . JESUS TEACHES HOW THE SPIRIT OF UNFORGIVENESS (THE TORTURERS. . .) EXACTS ITS TOLL ON OUR BODIES, MINDS, AND EMOTIONS. FINALLY, EVERY "KINGDOM" PERSON IS ADVISED TO SUSTAIN A FORGIVING HEART TOWARD ALL OTHER PERSONS.
—Jack Hayford, "Kingdom Dynamics" at Matthew 18:18–35, *New Spirit-Filled Life® Bible*

3.   The apostle Paul wrote Ephesians and Colossians at the same time, from the same jail cell in Rome, and sent them by the same messenger to cities in Asia Minor (Eph. 6:21, 22; Col. 4:7–9). Not surprisingly, Ephesians and Colossians

are similar to one another in structure and content. Read Ephesians 4:32 and Colossians 3:13 and answer the following questions.

As you reflect on the forgiveness Christ has extended you, what are the characteristics of that forgiveness that stand out to you?

What kinds of characteristics do you think should mark the forgiveness Christ expects you to extend to others?

4. Colossians 3:13 mentions *bearing with one another*. We are to put up with the annoyances and unintentional offenses that come from the people around us. Forgiveness is the grace we extend to those who use words and deeds to hurt us *on purpose*. Often we call it forgiveness when we put up with unintentional hurts, so we don't have to face the reality that we aren't forgiving those who intentionally hurt us. Make a list of the people in your family, neighborhood, church, workplace, and elsewhere who have intentionally hurt you in some way. Put a star by the names of those you have trouble forgiving.

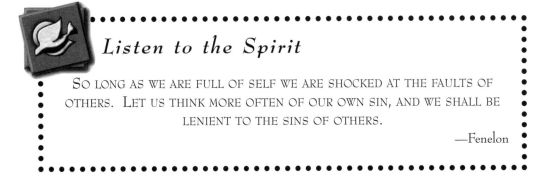

Listen to the Spirit

SO LONG AS WE ARE FULL OF SELF WE ARE SHOCKED AT THE FAULTS OF OTHERS. LET US THINK MORE OFTEN OF OUR OWN SIN, AND WE SHALL BE LENIENT TO THE SINS OF OTHERS.

—Fenelon

5. Take as much time as you need to in order to write a prayer telling God very honestly how you feel about forgiving the people whose names you starred in item 4. If you cannot forgive them or don't know how to forgive them, schedule an appointment with your pastor or other trusted spiritual leader to talk and pray your way to victory in this matter. This is too important to ignore or postpone to "a more convenient time." If you have forgiven everyone on your list, write your thanksgiving to God for the forgiveness you have received and that you have been able to give.

A New Song

Merciful Father, I can't do this. Sometimes my heart is numb and I don't even feel the pain. Then I can deny anyone hurt me. Other times I give You the offenses and give the offenders forgiveness, but eventually I take the offenses back from Your hands. Why do I clutch them to my heart where they poison my peace and destroy my joy? I will give the offenses to You and forgive the offenders over and over until I am free of them. Free to be more like You. In Jesus' name. Amen.

FRIENDSHIP

HOW ARE YOU doing in regard to friendship? Some people make and keep friends easily; some do not. Still others may even be afraid of vulnerability or intimacy, and for that reason, choose not to develop genuine friendships. Regardless of your situation, the Book of Proverbs offers practical wisdom for building and maintaining godly friendships.

1. Several proverbs describe the way friendships should function. What quality of friendships do these groups of proverbs highlight?

Proverbs 16:28; 17:9

Proverbs 17:17; 18:24; 27:6, 10

Proverbs 27:9, 17

Proverbs 25:20; 26:18, 19; 27:14

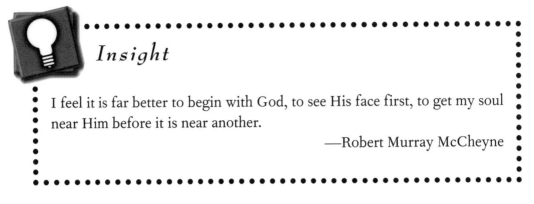

Insight

I feel it is far better to begin with God, to see His face first, to get my soul near Him before it is near another.

—Robert Murray McCheyne

2.   David and Jonathan probably enjoyed the most famous friendship in the Bible. It survived the hostility of Jonathan's father, Saul and the separation of the friends when King Saul forced David to flee for his life. Jonathan would not abandon his friendship with David even though David's rise to prominence meant Jonathan would never be king. Read these Scripture passages and answer the following questions based on them (1 Sam 18:1–4; 20:12–17, 30–34, 41, 42; 23:18).

What is captured about friendship when the Bible says Jonathan loved David as his own soul?

What was added to the natural affection of these friends by their formal promises to care for one another?

Do you think the open displays of affection and emotion strengthened or weakened the friendship of David and Jonathan? Why?

What do you imagine it meant to these two men during the time they were separated by King Saul's anger to know that they were friends who had made solemn promises to one another?

What it might have meant to David

What it might have meant to Jonathan

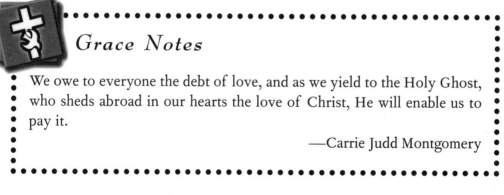

Grace Notes

We owe to everyone the debt of love, and as we yield to the Holy Ghost, who sheds abroad in our hearts the love of Christ, He will enable us to pay it.

—Carrie Judd Montgomery

3. Give some prayerful thought to this question before writing anything down. What has been the most intentional friendship (outside of marriage) in your life—the friendship you talked most about with your friend,

the friendship that may have involved promises, the friendship that got you through a tough time, etc.? What made (makes) it a strong friendship?

4. Circle the letters of the qualities that are strengths you bring to your friendships. Underline the letters of the qualities in which you are weak as a friend.

a. I am loyal.

b. I keep confidences.

c. I am a good listener.

d. I encourage my friends.

e. When necessary, I rebuke my friends.

f. I am happy when my friends succeed.

g. I have a good sense of humor.

h. I am a peacemaker.

i. I accept counsel and rebuke.

j. I confront problems and resolve conflicts.

k. I am generous.

l. I am hospitable.

m. Other:

A New Song

Loyal Lord, grant me a steadfast heart that I can be true. Thank You for Jesus, my Friend who sticks closer than a brother. Renew my mind and heart by Your Word and Spirit so that I can become a friend like Jesus. Teach me to give myself to my friends, and to receive their love in return as precious gifts. In Jesus' name. Amen.

5. Meditate awhile on the fruit of the Spirit and write a sentence or two about what each of these should contribute to your friendships.

    a. Love

    b. Joy

    c. Peace

    d. Long-suffering

    e. Kindness

    f. Goodness

    g. Faithfulness

    h. Gentleness

    i. Self-control

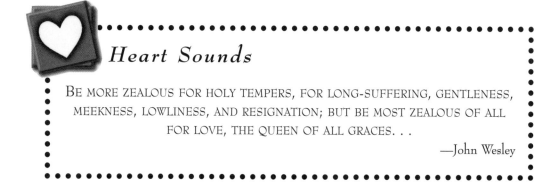

Heart Sounds

BE MORE ZEALOUS FOR HOLY TEMPERS, FOR LONG-SUFFERING, GENTLENESS, MEEKNESS, LOWLINESS, AND RESIGNATION; BUT BE MOST ZEALOUS OF ALL FOR LOVE, THE QUEEN OF ALL GRACES. . .

—John Wesley

6. Write the name of your best friend in the space below. Think about the value of this friendship to you. If you were going to tell this friend what he/she means to you, what would you say? Would you highlight character traits, shared experiences, or benefits of the friendship to you? Write your comments after your friend's name. Consider sharing this with your friend.

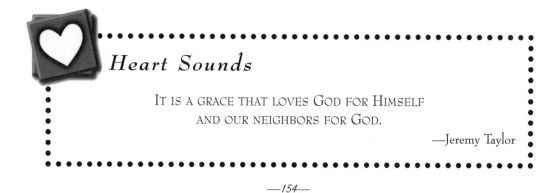

Heart Sounds

IT IS A GRACE THAT LOVES GOD FOR HIMSELF AND OUR NEIGHBORS FOR GOD.

—Jeremy Taylor

THE GOLDEN RULE

MOST OF US expect too much from our family and friends. We look at relation-ships in terms of what we're getting from them instead of what we're giving to them. Jesus taught us what we call "the Golden Rule"—to weave a fabric of interdependence into all our relationships. "Do unto others as you would have others do unto you," He commanded. When we live like that in relationship with the people in our sphere of influence, we treat people well proactively. Too often we "Do unto others just as others do unto us," but Jesus never wanted us to live by keeping score—loving our friends, hating our enemies, and getting even with those who mistreat us.

1. More often than not, the Golden Rule is not the primary principle govern-ing our interpersonal relationships. Circle the letter of the following state-ment that best expresses the primary attitude with which you approach interactions with people.

    a. I don't want to get hurt, so I don't reveal much of myself.

    b. I want to be liked, so I try to please.

    c. I like to listen, so I get people to tell me about themselves.

    d. I need to be in control, so I dominate or manipulate.

    e. I love communication, so I'll talk about anything.

    f. I like to do things. I'd rather not talk but share activities.

    g. I am insecure. I gossip about and criticize others.

    h. I need to impress people, even if I have to exaggerate the truth.

    i. I love people and enjoy encouraging them.

    j. Other:

2. What would you say is the greatest strength of your interpersonal relationship skills, and how does this strength manifest itself? What is the greatest weakness in your relational skills, and what strength would you like to see replace this weakness?

Greatest strength

Greatest weakness

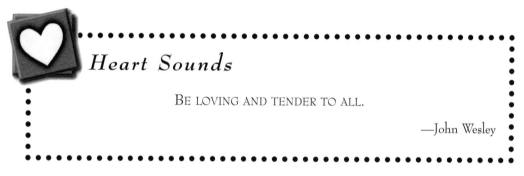

Heart Sounds

BE LOVING AND TENDER TO ALL.

—John Wesley

3. The Golden Rule appears twice in the recorded teachings of Jesus (Matt. 7:12; Luke 6:31). In both cases it summarizes a topic Jesus was teaching His disciples. Read the following passages and report what Jesus was teaching and how the Golden Rule is an application of that subject.

Matthew 7:9–12

Luke 6:27–31

4. Toward the end of Ephesians 4, the apostle Paul focused on how to treat people in a passage that applies the Golden Rule. Read Ephesians 4:25–27, 29–32. How did Paul apply the Golden Rule to each of these areas of interpersonal relationships?

Honesty

Anger Management

Speech

Kindness

Forgiveness

5. How does each of these impact our success or failure in following the spiritual instructions of Ephesians 4:25–27, 29–32?

The devil

The Holy Spirit

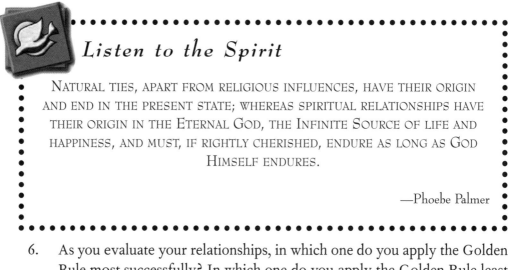

Listen to the Spirit

NATURAL TIES, APART FROM RELIGIOUS INFLUENCES, HAVE THEIR ORIGIN AND END IN THE PRESENT STATE; WHEREAS SPIRITUAL RELATIONSHIPS HAVE THEIR ORIGIN IN THE ETERNAL GOD, THE INFINITE SOURCE OF LIFE AND HAPPINESS, AND MUST, IF RIGHTLY CHERISHED, ENDURE AS LONG AS GOD HIMSELF ENDURES.

—Phoebe Palmer

6. As you evaluate your relationships, in which one do you apply the Golden Rule most successfully? In which one do you apply the Golden Rule least successfully?

Most successfully

Least successfully

7. Why do you think you have so much trouble applying the Golden Rule to the relationship you identified as a problem in item 6?

8. What attitudes and behaviors need to change in order for you to treat this person as you want to be treated? In what ways do you need to yield to the Holy Spirit in this relationship so you stop grieving Him?

Listen to the Spirit

LOVE IS THE KEY.
JOY IS LOVE SINGING.
PEACE IS LOVE RESTING.
LONG-SUFFERING IS LOVE ENDURING.
KINDNESS IS LOVE'S TOUCH.
GOODNESS IS LOVE'S CHARACTER.
FAITHFULNESS IS LOVE'S HABIT.
GENTLENESS IS LOVE'S SELF-FORGETFULNESS.
SELF-CONTROL IS LOVE HOLDING THE REINS.
—Donald Grey Barnhouse

IRON SHARPENS IRON

WE WANT OUR relationships to be filled with grace, but from time to time, we find ourselves needing to speak "the truth in love" (Eph. 4:15). Our communication may be as simple as telling a person that her lipstick is smeared or that his shirt is not buttoned properly. At other times, our confrontation may be more serious and will need to be preceded and accompanied by much prayer. Believers all live in the family of God together and as we learn to live in healthy, godly relationships, and communicate clearly, individuals grow and the body is edified.

1. Proverbs 17:17 reads, *As iron sharpens iron, so a man sharpens the countenance of his friend*. Circle the letter of the following statement that comes closest to expressing your reaction to that proverb.

    a. It sounds like stubborn guys butting heads over everything.

    b. I think of two people standing toe-to-toe, arguing until sparks fly, and loving it.

    c. I think of friends who, over a long time, slowly benefit one another through a lot of give and take.

    d. I'm afraid of that kind of friendship. I'm more jelly than iron. I can neither take it nor dish it out.

    e. Other:

2. As you think back over your life, who from your family, friends, workplace, military experience, athletic career, etc. has had the most positive impact on you by being a friend who dared to knock off a few of your rough edges? How did this person function as iron sharpening iron for you?

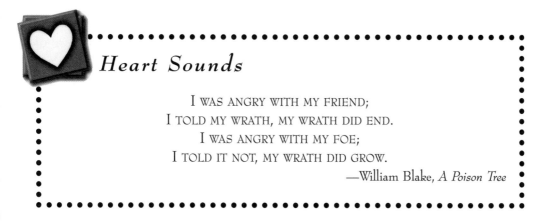

Heart Sounds

I WAS ANGRY WITH MY FRIEND;
I TOLD MY WRATH, MY WRATH DID END.
I WAS ANGRY WITH MY FOE;
I TOLD IT NOT, MY WRATH DID GROW.

—William Blake, *A Poison Tree*

3. Proverbs 27:6 says, *Faithful are the wounds of a friend, but the kisses of an enemy are deceitful.* What do you think that proverb means?

4. Recall a time when a friend had the courage to say something to you that was hard for you to hear but necessary. How did you react immediately and after you had time to reflect?

5. Recall a time when you wounded a friend with your words in order to help that person. Would you handle the situation differently if you could do it again? What did you learn about friendship through this encounter?

6. According to Proverbs 28:23, *He who rebukes a man will find more favor afterward than he who flatters with the tongue.* Put a plus sign (+) in front of the characteristics that will help the truth of this proverb work in a relationship. Put a minus sign (–) in front of the relational traits that will prevent the truth of this proverb from operating.

    a. Both people are secure in their relationship with the Lord.

    b. One person is controlling and the other is afraid.

    c. Both people are selfish.

    d. Both people freely express their opinions and feelings.

    e. One or both people are emotionally needy.

    f. One or both people will accept temporary disruption of the relationship in order to gain a stronger friendship in the long term.

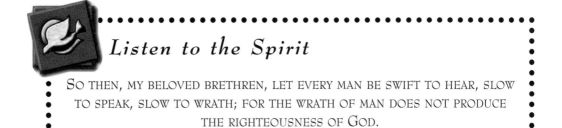

Listen to the Spirit

SO THEN, MY BELOVED BRETHREN, LET EVERY MAN BE SWIFT TO HEAR, SLOW TO SPEAK, SLOW TO WRATH; FOR THE WRATH OF MAN DOES NOT PRODUCE THE RIGHTEOUSNESS OF GOD.

—James 1:19, 20

7. In the space below, write a prayer in which you ask the Lord to empower you by His Spirit to receive rebuke in a way that strengthens you and honors Him.

8. Select the statement that best describes your attitude toward confrontation in relationships. In the space after the options, write your thoughts on how you could become more effective in "sharpening" your relationships.

    a. I'm too fearful of losing relationships to confront friends or family members.

    b. I'm too lazy to do the hard work of confronting friends or family.

    c. My temper keeps me from being objective and constructive in confrontational situations.

    d. I have been effective in confrontation but didn't enjoy it.

    e. I may enjoy confrontation a little too much.

    f. I need to develop my ability to receive confrontation before thinking of initiating it.

A New Song

Almighty Father, whose Son is the perfect Word, full of grace and truth, protect my words. When I should confront, give me courage to speak the truth and give compassion to do so graciously. May Your Spirit so guide and guard my tongue that You will be pleased and honored. In Jesus' name. Amen.

CONFLICT RESOLUTION

STRONG RELATIONSHIPS CAN weather storms. When conflicts arise, they must be dealt with in a biblical way. The lesson following will help you develop skills for healthy resolution that should result in the strengthening of the individuals involved and the relationship.

1.   Some people relish conflict; some dread it; some accept it as a necessary evil of life. Which of these best describes you in resolving a conflict?

     a.   A chameleon.

     b.   A scolding squirrel.

     c.   A hummingbird that flits around but never lands.

     d.   A guide dog for the blind.

     e.   A lion pouncing on its prey.

2.   Describe a bad conflict resolution experience you had, either as the initiator or recipient. What made this confrontation a failure?

3. Describe a successful conflict resolution experience you had, either as the initiator or recipient. What made this confrontation effective?

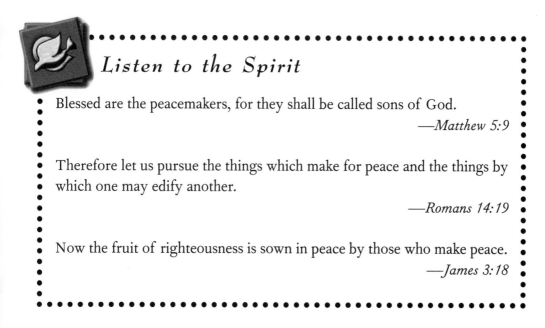

Listen to the Spirit

Blessed are the peacemakers, for they shall be called sons of God.

—*Matthew 5:9*

Therefore let us pursue the things which make for peace and the things by which one may edify another.

—*Romans 14:19*

Now the fruit of righteousness is sown in peace by those who make peace.

—*James 3:18*

4. Jesus gave pretty specific instructions on resolving conflict. He addressed situations caused by your mistakes and situations caused by someone else's mistakes. What is your responsibility in each of these situations?

A conflict that is your fault (Matt. 5:23, 24)

A conflict that is the other person's fault (Matt. 18:15–17)

5.   You can't force someone to resolve a conflict with you. You can only do what the Scriptures instruct you to do. Then the responsibility for any continuing disruption is not yours but the party unwilling to reconcile. Put a star by the response in the following list that you want to make with the help of God's Spirit when someone refuses to reconcile with you. Put a minus sign (–) by the bad response(s) you tend to make in the flesh but want to resist.

    a.   I'll give you the silent treatment.

    b.   I'll pray for you and wait for future reconciliation.

    c.   I'll tell everyone that you refused biblical reconciliation.

    d.   I'll treat you as a friend in the hopes that you will respond to love.

    e.   I'll treat you as an enemy and try to get even with you.

    f.   I'll quietly get a large number of people praying for the reconciliation.

6.   In addition to conflicts between people, the Bible addresses the conflict caused within the church by known sin in a believer's life. Read Galatians 6:1 and James 5:19, 20. How do these passages advise you to proceed when you are concerned for a brother entangled in sin?

Heart Sounds

Jesus told His disciples,

"Go your way; behold, I send you out as lambs among wolves. . . . But whatever house you enter, first say, 'Peace be to this house.' And if a son of peace is there, your peace will rest on it; if not, it will return to you."

—Luke 10:3, 5, 6

7. How do you think a person should handle his/her inner turmoil regarding, for example, a father who has been unfaithful in his marriage?

What does he/she need to do with regards to forgiveness?

How should he/she apply the Golden Rule?

What might he/she do in terms of conflict resolution?

8. What unresolved or partially resolved conflicts hang over your network of relationships? Spend some time in prayer about the most serious of these and write some biblical steps you should take to attempt to resolve this conflict.

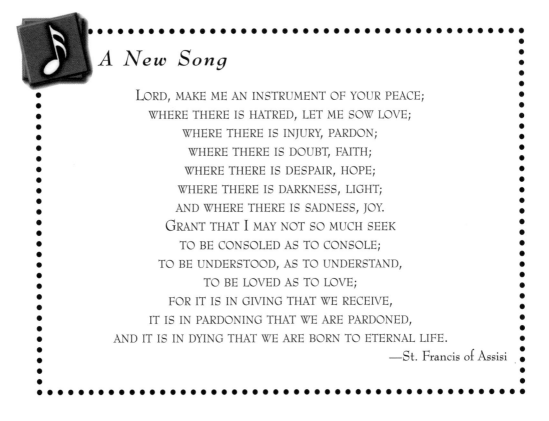

A New Song

LORD, MAKE ME AN INSTRUMENT OF YOUR PEACE;
WHERE THERE IS HATRED, LET ME SOW LOVE;
WHERE THERE IS INJURY, PARDON;
WHERE THERE IS DOUBT, FAITH;
WHERE THERE IS DESPAIR, HOPE;
WHERE THERE IS DARKNESS, LIGHT;
AND WHERE THERE IS SADNESS, JOY.
GRANT THAT I MAY NOT SO MUCH SEEK
TO BE CONSOLED AS TO CONSOLE;
TO BE UNDERSTOOD, AS TO UNDERSTAND,
TO BE LOVED AS TO LOVE;
FOR IT IS IN GIVING THAT WE RECEIVE,
IT IS IN PARDONING THAT WE ARE PARDONED,
AND IT IS IN DYING THAT WE ARE BORN TO ETERNAL LIFE.

—St. Francis of Assisi

CHAPTER 7

SPIRIT-FILLED LEADERSHIP

The Bible is full of leaders: Moses, Joshua, Samuel, David, Nehemiah, Peter, and a host of others. Some were soldiers, some were priests, some were prophets, and some were kings. But all of them were simply shadows of the greatest leader of all—King Jesus, who is still ruling today.

In God's kingdom, there are both anointed leaders and anointed followers. That's why 1 Corinthians 12:12 says, "the body is one and has many members." All of us together compose the beautiful body of Jesus Christ, who is our Head. Perhaps you know already that you are called by God to lead in some capacity. Perhaps you know you have the gift to serve, and are called to be a faithful, excellent follower. Then again, maybe you are not sure yet exactly where your place in the body is. Whatever the case, this chapter will help. If you are a leader, it can inform the way you lead and guide you into more Spirit-empowered leadership. If you are a follower, it can help you understand leadership in such a way that you can flourish as a servant. And if you are not certain, you may discover your calling in the following pages. Are you ready to answer God's unique call to you?

THE HOLINESS OF GOD

HOLY CALLINGS ARE not exclusive to pastors or those in professional leadership roles. Everyone is called by God for a specific purpose, and there is biblical and theological support for the fact that a divine calling and mandate rests upon the life of every believer.

1.   We have a tendency to want precise direction from God about the details of our daily lives. If He would only make all our decisions and plans, we wouldn't have to take responsibility for doing the hard human work of thinking, weighing options, making choices, and planning or the harder spiritual work of seeking God's guidance through prayer and reliance on the Holy Spirit during the whole process. Look up the following Scriptures and summarize the teaching of each regarding the call of God to every believer in Jesus.

Matthew 9:13

Romans 1:7

Romans 8:28–30

1 Corinthians 1:2, 9

1 Corinthians 1:26–31

1 Corinthians 7:15

Galatians 5:13

Colossians 3:15

1 Thessalonians 2:12

1 Thessalonians 4:7

1 Timothy 6:12

1 Peter 2:9

1 Peter 2:20, 21

1 Peter 3:8, 9

1 Peter 5:10

2.   Write a brief paragraph expressing the general concepts of our calling in Christ contained in the passages above.

3.   Which of the following statements best describes your relationship to leadership in your church?

   a.   I believe God has called me to leadership in Christ's church.

   b.   I am a leader in the church but I can't say I have been called by God.

   c.   I am an administrative leader but not a spiritual leader.

   d.   I am confused about leadership and the idea of a divine call.

   e.   I don't want to be a leader. I get asked to lead, but I don't want to.

   f.   I am not a leader. I am a behind-the-scenes kind of worker.

   g.   I am uninvolved in leadership or ministry.

   h.   Other:

   The Latin verb that means "to call" is *vocare*, from which English derives the noun *vocation*. By derivation a "vocation" is not a career, an occupation, or a job. It is a calling. In the past, the noun "vocation" was reserved for noble professions, such as the pastorate, medicine, education, statesmanship, and law, to indicate that God directed people into these careers in a special way.

4.   In the following Bible passages, God called people into leadership in various ways. Read the passages and indicate in the space provided, how God's call came to the leader(s) involved.

Isaiah 6:1–9

Acts 6:2–6

Acts 22:1–21

Romans 12:3–8

Titus 1:5–9

Insight

The godly leader "hears" God; that is, his or her spirit is tuned to the promptings and lessons of the Holy Spirit. . . . Jesus emphasized that leadership in His church would always lead and be based not on man's ability to reason things out as much as on his readiness and receptivity to hear God through "revelation knowledge," the things that God unfolds by the work of the Holy Spirit (Eph. 1:17, 18; 3:14–19).

—Jamie Buckingham, "Traits of Spiritual Leadership,"
Hayford's Bible Handbook

5.   The biblical evidence does not suggest that every leader will hear the same "call." Some calls are dramatic, others quiet. Some are public, others private. Some come through supernatural means, some through human agents, and some through both. Some come when the leaders recognize their gifts, others before. All leaders have to open the ears of their spirits before they can hear the voice of God (1 Kin. 19:11–13).

What "interference" from inside one's head or heart could keep a person from hearing God's call to leadership?

What "interference" from the world and the devil could keep a person from hearing God's call to leadership?

How do you think a person keeps his or her spiritual ears open to hear God's call to be a leader or to hear His guidance once one is in leadership?

The passages involving selecting leaders in Acts 6 and appointing leaders in Titus 1 do not mention a call from God for those leaders. Ephesians 4:11–16 indicates that Christ "gives" leaders of all types to His church. The people rather than their skills are hand-picked gifts from the Lord, the Head of the body, to the church. Since "calling" is a biblical synonym for "choosing," leaders of this type receive their call when they realize the Lord has chosen them to lead.

A call from God is a crucial reference point during the inevitable struggles and doubts that accompany the responsibilities of leadership. Leaders who can only look back to personal decisions to accept responsibility have no reference point beyond themselves. Those leaders are vulnerable to discouragement and self-doubt. Leaders called by God have a reference point in the purposes of the Father, the kingdom of the Son, and the leading of the Holy Spirit. Those leaders can say with the apostle Paul, *For if I preach the gospel, I have nothing to boast of, for necessity is laid upon me; yes, woe is me if I do not preach the gospel!* (1 Cor. 9:16).

6. Take some time to reflect over the period of your Christian walk with the Lord. Meditate on the ways He has led you to make decisions, the times He has steered the course of your life into new channels, the people He has employed to influence you, and the abilities and education He has given you. What do all these factors suggest is God's calling for your life—whether it be a calling to leadership or some other role? What new insights have you gained through this study?

GIFTED FOR LEADERSHIP

"AREN'T CALLING AND gifting the same thing?" you may wonder. Sometimes people think that identifying their spiritual gifts will tell them whether or not they are called to leadership. But, such an idea could become a formula, and every time we reduce God's activity to some simple formula, we omit something really important. We can never put Him in our tidy little boxes, so let's further explore the relationship between gifting and calling.

1. Circle the letter of the following statement that best expresses your current understanding of the topic of spiritual gifts.

    a. I have training on spiritual gifts and know what mine is/are.

    b. I have read and heard of spiritual gifts but I'm still confused on which I have.

    c. I don't know the difference between spiritual gifts, natural abilities, and personality characteristics.

    d. I expect this all to be over my head.

    e. I think people make too big a deal of spiritual gifts.

    f. Other:

Insight

We find Romans 12:3–8 describing gifts given by God as Father. They seem to characterize basic "motivations," that is, inherent tendencies that characterize each different person by reason of the Creator's unique workmanship in their initial gifting. . . . Second, in 1 Corinthians 12:7–11, the nine gifts of the Holy Spirit are listed. Their purpose is specific—to "profit" the body of the church. . . . They are not to be merely acknowledged in a passive way, but rather are to be actively welcomed and expected (1 Cor. 13:1; 14:1). Third, the gifts which the Son of God has given are pivotal in assuring that the first two categories of gifts are applied in the body of the church. Ephesians 4:7–17 . . . indicates the "office gifts" Christ has placed in the church along with their purpose. . . . [This distinction] prevents us from confusing our foundational motivation in life and service for God with our purposeful quest for and openness to His Holy Spirit's full resources and power for service and ministry.

—Paul Walker, "Holy Spirit Gifts and Power,",
New Spirit-Filled Life® Bible

2. Read Romans 12:3–8, the passage referred to in the accompanying *Insight* as describing the motivational gifts given by God the Father. If these gifts provide "inherent tendencies that characterize each different person," what kind of leadership do you think a person with each of these gifts would tend to exercise?

Prophecy

Ministry (Service)

Teaching

Exhortation

Giving

Administration

Showing mercy

3. Which of these motivational gifts and its impact on leadership comes closest to describing you? Why? (If you are undecided or confused by this assignment, ask your pastor, small group leader, or trusted mature friend for their observations on which of these motivational gifts comes closest to describing you.)

Heart Sounds

4. Read 1 Corinthians 12:7–11 where the nine gifts of the Holy Spirit are enumerated. The earlier *Insights* feature indicates these are gifts the Spirit gives for the building up of the body of Christ. They are service-oriented gifts, given by the Spirit at or subsequent to salvation, for use in the church. They are not trophies to put on a shelf, but tools to work with. Underline the gifts in the following list (*New Spirit-Filled Life® Bible,* pp. 1856–57) that you would like to have. Circle the one(s) you think you do have.

   a. Word of Wisdom—Spirit-induced sense of divine direction on how to act

   b. Word of Knowledge—Spirit-aided insight into the nature of God's will and plan

   c. Faith—Spirit-given ability to trust God and combat unbelief

   d. Gifts of Healing—Spirit-based ability to participate in God's healing work in the lives of people

   e. Working of Miracles—Spirit-energized ability to combat evil and display God's power

   f. Prophecy—Spirit-based proclamation of God's will for a situation

   g. Discerning of Spirits—Spirit-aided insight into spiritual forces at work in a given situation

   h. Different Kinds of Tongues—Spirit-induced utterances in a language unknown to the speaker

   i. Interpretation of Tongues—Spirit-given ability to translate utterances in unknown tongues

5. What implications do you think your underlined and circled gifts have for you as a leader? What do you think the Holy Spirit wants to do through the "tools" He has entrusted to you? (Once again, if you are uncertain of your gifts, invite someone else who has spiritual maturity and wisdom to help you assess yourself.)

6. Obviously, not everyone is meant to be a leader. However, we often limit leadership in our minds to the highly visible spokespeople of formal organizations. Leadership is the exercise of influence within a formal or informal group to direct the collective energies of the group to establish or accomplish its goals. Many people who don't think they are leaders lead effectively in their families, small groups, Sunday school classes, clubs, athletic teams, neighborhood associations, PTAs, and workplace groups. What are your greatest success and worst failure as a leader at any level of responsibility?

Greatest Success

Worst Failure

7. What would you imagine your church leadership prospects are for the future? What in your gift and calling mix makes you think this?

A New Song

Thank You, heavenly Father, that You and the Son and the Spirit decide who should lead and how they should lead in the church of Jesus Christ. Grant me the humility that my ego isn't threatened if You don't want me to lead and the courage that my knees won't knock if You do.

Lord God, help me to be about the business of obeying Your Word, renewing my mind, communing with Your Spirit, fellowshipping with Your children, and rejoicing in Jesus. May Your grace and peace rule my heart. Whether I lead or follow in the church, may it be done as a disciple of my Lord and Savior. In Jesus' name. Amen.

PASSION AND LEADERSHIP

ONE OF THE leadership buzzwords at the beginning of the twenty-first century is "passion." In the church, discussions on "passion" have caused leaders to take seriously the deep-seated interests and desires God has placed in their hearts. What a leader is passionate about often determines the focus and style of that leader's service in the body of Christ. A gifted administrator who is passionate about protecting unborn infants may find the greatest fulfillment managing a crisis pregnancy center. A gifted administrator who has a passion for evangelizing China might be very frustrated managing that crisis pregnancy center, even though he or she believes strongly in its objectives.

1. It is sometimes possible to observe leaders in action and figure out the things for which they feel strongly. Below are three New Testament leaders and their spiritual gifts as identified in the Bible. Read the passages associated with each and identify what you think were their individual passions. How would you expect each leader's passion to affect his leadership?

Paul, apostle to the Gentiles (Acts 16:6–10; 19:21; Rom. 15:20; 2 Cor. 10:15, 16)

Barnabas, prophet and teacher (Acts 4:36, 37; 9:26, 27; 15:36–40)

Peter, apostle to the Jews (Acts 2:17–21; 10:36–43; 2 Pet. 1:16–19)

2. A person's passion may relate to a group of people, a geographical region, or an activity. Look through the lists below and underline all in which you have strong interest. Then go back and put a star in front of the ones about which you are passionate.

Group of People	Geographical Region	Activity
Children	Home Town	Music
Teenagers	North America	Drama
Single Adults	South	AmericaArt
Adults	Europe	Writing
Older Adults	Asia	Medicine
Mentally Challenged	Africa	Law
Physically Challenged	Australia	Agriculture
Unborn Children	Pacific Islands	Counseling
Other	Other	Other

Heart Sounds

God has called us to shine, just as much as Daniel was sent into Babylon to shine. Let no one say that he cannot shine because he has not so much influence as some others may have. What God wants you to do is to use the influence you have. Daniel probably did not have much influence down in Babylon at first, but God soon gave him more because he was faithful and used what he had.

—Dwight L. Moody

3. What roles in your church or other Christian ministries can you imagine feeling excitement toward on the basis of the passion(s) you identified in exercise 2? Take into account your gifts, educational background, and personal situation.

4. As you reflect on your temperament and background, how would you say the Holy Spirit managed to build this passion into your make-up? Why do you think He wanted you to care for this more than other things?

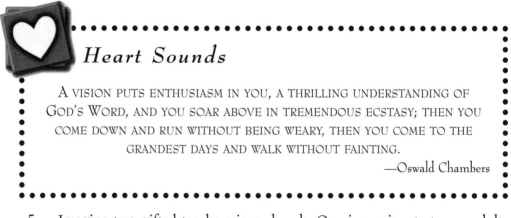

Heart Sounds

A VISION PUTS ENTHUSIASM IN YOU, A THRILLING UNDERSTANDING OF GOD'S WORD, AND YOU SOAR ABOVE IN TREMENDOUS ECSTASY; THEN YOU COME DOWN AND RUN WITHOUT BEING WEARY, THEN YOU COME TO THE GRANDEST DAYS AND WALK WITHOUT FAINTING.

—Oswald Chambers

5. Imagine two gifted teachers in a church. One is passionate to see adults reach mature Christian discipleship. The other is passionate to see young children actively discovering the foundational truths of faith in Jesus.

How different might the teaching style of these two gifted teachers be?

How might these gifted teachers misunderstand one another because of their different passions?

6. Sometimes divergent passions divide churches and Christian friends. Pro-life activists can't understand how any committed Christian could be less committed to the cause than they are. Passionate evangelists question the faith of brothers and sisters who are afraid of confrontational witnessing. Generally, we all need to be more understanding of the range of passions the Spirit of God has placed in the hearts of God's people. Circle the letter(s) of the following Spirit-given passion(s) for which you need to be more understanding.

    a. Drama
    b. World missions
    c. Apologetics
    d. Child evangelism
    e. Camping
    f. Athletic ministries
    g. Political activism
    h. Pro-life activism
    i. Prison ministry
    j. Any style of music you don't like
    k. Older adults
    l. Babies
    m. Participatory learning
    n. Lecture-style learning
    o. Other:

Insight

We may affirm absolutely that nothing great in the world has been accomplished without passion.

—Friedrich Hegel, *Philosophy of History*

7. In 1 Corinthians 12:4–6, the apostle Paul wrote, *There are diversities of gifts, but the same Spirit. There are differences of ministries, but the same Lord. And there are diversities of activities, but it is the same God who works all in all.* The Holy Spirit equips each believer with a divinely enhanced ability. The Lord Jesus sovereignly directs the church into its ministries, or programs. God the Father involves Himself with "activities," *energemata* in Greek. The "energizings"—the passions—are from Him. As you think what your passion in ministry may be, how does it influence your thinking on your leadership potential?

1	2	3	4	5	6	7	8	9	10
None		A Little		Some		Quite a Bit			Lots

CHARACTERS FOR LEADERSHIP

SPIRIT-FILLED LEADERSHIP will be godly leadership. Godly leadership will be leadership characterized by integrity. Integrity deals with more than finances and truth telling. Integrity includes how a leader treats people, how openly a leader communicates with followers, and how humbly a leader exercises authority. We tend to rate a leader's success in terms of the latest best-seller on management theory. God rates leaders in terms of the Beatitudes and the Fruit of the Spirit.

1. Read through the following list of character traits that might be expected of leaders. Circle the four that you think are most important. In the space below the list, explain why you chose the ones you did.

   a. Sense of humor   i. Reputation

   b. Honesty   j. Peace-loving

   c. Thrift   k. Generosity

   d. Charisma   l. Experience

   e. Discernment   m. Joy

   f. Graciousness   n. Serenity

   g. Self-discipline   o. Other:

   h. Godliness

2. James 3:1 reads, *My brethren, let not many of you become teachers, knowing that we shall receive a stricter judgment.* Circle the letter of the following statement that you think best explains what James had in mind when he wrote this.

   a. Because leaders are telling people what to do and how to live, they are obligated to set the pace in character and conduct.

b. Leaders are first-class Christians, so their conduct must be better than that of second-class Christians.

c. Responsibility comes with authority. God rewards those leaders who meet increased responsibilities and punishes those who fail to meet those responsibilities.

d. People who aren't leaders shouldn't covet authority because leadership is more hard work than glamour.

e. The biggest challenge and responsibility of leadership, and the most likely source of trouble, is oral communication.

f. Other:

Insight

The qualifications for church leaders . . . do not emphasize family line or some past rite as the OT priesthood did. Instead the focus is on the leader's certified and sustained ethical character. . . . The basis for continual ministry is continual commitment to character. If a leader falls from these ethical standards, he or she should accept removal from leadership until an appropriate season of reverifying of character can be fulfilled.
—Jamie Buckingham, "Kingdom Dynamics" at 1 Timothy 3:1–13,
New Spirit-Filled Life® Bible

3. Given the warning of James 3:1, why do you think anyone would want to be a leader in the church and face such accountability?

Listen to the Spirit

Leaders are judged with a higher standard than those who follow. . . . Leaders in the kingdom, however, are judged not so much by what they accomplish as by the character they reveal—who they <u>are</u> before what they <u>do</u>. This high standard applied not so much to the leader's achievements as to the condition of his or her heart and spirit. It is possible to have grand accomplishments and even orthodox behavior but still manifest a loveless, ungodly spirit.

—Jamie Buckingham, "Traits of Spiritual Leadership,"
Hayford's Bible Handbook

4. Several New Testament passages describe the kind of character various groups were looking for as they considered possible leaders. Read the following passages that concern the character of leaders. Don't just list the traits mentioned in the biblical texts. Think of each passage and write one or two sentences in your own words on the kind of person God wants to lead His church.

Acts 6:3, 6

1 Timothy 3:1–13; Titus 1:5–9

1 Timothy 6:3–12, 20, 21

Hebrews 13:7, 17

1 Peter 5:1–4

5. Circle the letter of the following statement that best expresses what you sense as the primary difference between the character expectations of God for leaders and the character expectations of the world.

    a.   God wants leaders who exemplify their product; the world wants leaders who can produce their product.

    b.   God and the world want the same kind of leader; the world just doesn't know why character and a servant heart are essential to effective leadership.

    c.   God wants leaders who motivate with love; the world wants leaders who motivate with power.

    d.   God wants leaders who rely on His Spirit; the world wants leaders who rely on themselves.

    e.   God wants leaders who are successful in all spheres of their lives; the world wants leaders who will neglect all other spheres of their lives.

    f.   Other:

Listen to the Spirit

Godly leaders lead by inspiration. Deborah convinced her followers to extend themselves beyond their own vision. The inspirational leader provides a model of integrity and courage and sets a high standard of performance.

—Jamie Buckingham, "Traits of Spiritual Leadership,"
Hayford's Bible Handbook

6. Not everyone is a leader. Not every leader exercises authority well. Circle the letter of the following statement that best expresses the balance between leading and following in the organized activities of your life.

   a. I'm a lone wolf. I don't work well in groups.

   b. I tend to resent authority, but I keep my mouth shut and do what I'm told.

   c. I feel like I could lead better than most of my bosses, but nobody has ever given me the chance to be in charge.

   d. I follow orders precisely and find satisfaction in doing as I'm told.

   e. I get along well with supervisors and sometimes make suggestions on how I think my tasks could be done better.

   f. I lead in major areas of my life, but I follow the lead of others in some areas,

   g. I tend to take leadership roles in all areas of my life.

   h. I need to lead. I don't like to be in settings where I'm not in control.

   i. Other:

7. Spend some time reflecting on your answer to item 6 and the things you have been thinking from this study on "Character for Leadership." Does your answer to item 6 suggest any character issues that you need to deal with as a follower or a leader? If so, what are they? If not, what positive things have you learned about yourself as a leader or a follower?

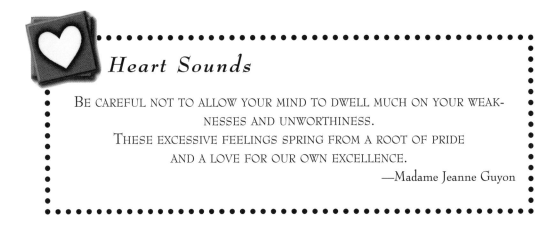

Heart Sounds

BE CAREFUL NOT TO ALLOW YOUR MIND TO DWELL MUCH ON YOUR WEAK-
NESSES AND UNWORTHINESS.
THESE EXCESSIVE FEELINGS SPRING FROM A ROOT OF PRIDE
AND A LOVE FOR OUR OWN EXCELLENCE.

—Madame Jeanne Guyon

SERVANT LEADERSHIP

SPIRIT-FILLED LEADERSHIP is servant leadership. Jesus loved to stand the logic of the world on its head. So He insisted that the leaders in the kingdom of God should be servants, even as the last shall be first and the least shall be the greatest. The term "minister" means servant, and "ministry" means service. Both are menial terms that have taken on high-sounding religious significance through the years. Even the phrase "servant leader" has become trite. Let's see if we can't freshen it up and make it sound radical again as it did in Jesus' day.

1. Jesus said, *"For even the Son of Man did not come to be served, but to serve, and to give His life a ransom for many"* (Mark 10:45). When you think of a servant leader, which of the following pictures comes to your mind?

    a. A waiter in a restaurant.

    b. An old-time doctor making a house call.

    c. An insurance salesman presenting his policy options.

    d. A ship's captain on his bridge at night.

    e. A corporate executive concerned about investors' dividends.

    f. Other:

2. Why did you choose the option you did in item 1? How does your selection illustrate the servant leadership you think Jesus had in mind?

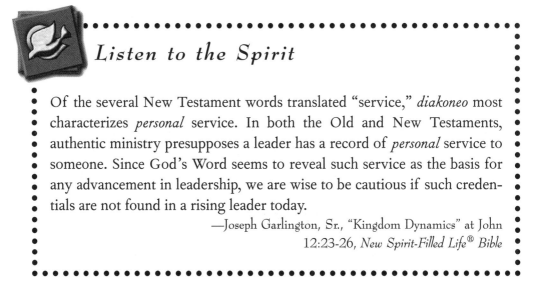

Listen to the Spirit

Of the several New Testament words translated "service," *diakoneo* most characterizes *personal* service. In both the Old and New Testaments, authentic ministry presupposes a leader has a record of *personal* service to someone. Since God's Word seems to reveal such service as the basis for any advancement in leadership, we are wise to be cautious if such credentials are not found in a rising leader today.

—Joseph Garlington, Sr., "Kingdom Dynamics" at John 12:23-26, *New Spirit-Filled Life*® *Bible*

3. The apostle Paul held up Jesus as the primary example of servant leadership in Philippians 2:5–11. We looked at this passage briefly on the fifth day of our study of holiness in chapter one. We were exploring humility and holiness at that point. Read this passage again and answer the following questions regarding servant leadership.

In what part of the personality does servant leadership begin (Phil. 2:5)?

What spiritual attitudes are necessary before a person can be a servant leader (Phil. 2:8)?

How did Jesus serve humanity (Phil. 2:6–8)?

What can leaders do to serve those they lead that reflects the attitudes and goals of Jesus?

4. Who have you known who followed the servant leader example of Jesus as described in Philippians 2? How did this person exemplify the mind of Jesus?

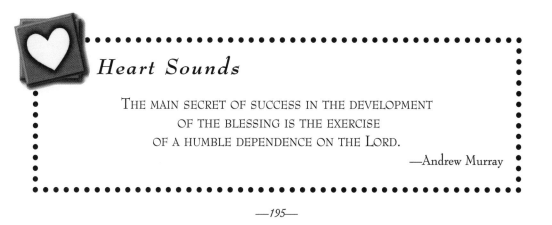

Heart Sounds

THE MAIN SECRET OF SUCCESS IN THE DEVELOPMENT
OF THE BLESSING IS THE EXERCISE
OF A HUMBLE DEPENDENCE ON THE LORD.

—Andrew Murray

5. The apostle Paul served many fledgling churches established during his missionary travels. He expressed the tenderest concerns for the Thessalonian believers, even though he only spent a few weeks with them (Acts 17:2). Paul compared his leadership of the Thessalonians to the nurture and guidance offered children by their parents. Read 1 Thessalonians 2:7–12.

What characteristics of a nursing mother did Paul use to illustrate his leadership among the Thessalonians (1 Thess. 2:7–9)?

How could you apply these maternal qualities to servant leadership in your church?

What characteristics of a father of older children did Paul use to illustrate his leadership among the Thessalonians (1 Thess. 2:10–12)?

How could you apply these paternal qualities to servant leadership in your church?

Insight

When the New Testament speaks of ministering to the saints, it means not primarily preaching to them but devoting time, trouble, and substance to giving them all the practical help possible. The essence of Christian service is loyalty to the king expressing itself in care for his servants (Matt. 25:31–46).

Only the Holy Spirit can create in us the kind of love toward our Savior that will overflow in imaginative sympathy and practical helpfulness towards His people. Unless the Spirit is training us in love, we are not fit persons to go to college or a training class to learn the know-how or particular branches of Christian work. Gifted leaders who are self-centered and loveless are a blight to the church rather than a blessing.

—Jamie Buckingham, "Traits of Spiritual Leadership,"
Hayford's Bible Handbook

6. Perhaps you wonder how a leader called by God, gifted by the Holy Spirit, and energized by passion to see the church move forward can be a servant leader. Consider the character and leadership of the Holy Spirit who came on Pentecost to give birth to the church of Jesus Christ, and you may better understand the leaders the Spirit empowers to direct that church.

The character of the Holy Spirit (Acts 2:2–4; 4:31; 1 Cor. 2:10, 11)

The mission of the Holy Spirit (John 16:7–14)

The humility of the Holy Spirit (John 16:13, 14; Eph. 4:30; 1 Thess. 5:19)

7. What has this study contributed to the growth of your understanding of Spirit-filled leadership?

GROWTH IN THE SPIRIT

In God, growth never stops. We never learn everything there is to learn about Him. We never run out of ways to serve Him. We can never find enough words to describe Him, and we can never worship Him enough. When we live the Spirit-filled life, our well of prayer, praise, and thanksgiving never runs dry. There is always something new to experience, always a fresh encounter to be had. That's the wonder of the Spirit of God.

Now that you have almost completed this workbook, this last chapter will be like a launch-pad, a place from which you can continue to grow and be strengthened because your foundation is firm. There is no end to what you will find as you continue to plumb the depths of God. Are you ready?

DAY 1 ENCOUNTER WITH THE SPIRIT

PAUL WALKER WRITES, "[The] Charismatic sees the baptism or infilling of the Holy Spirit as an experience subsequent to Christian conversion: one that comes through a process of yielding the complete person into the guidance and indwelling of the Holy Spirit. We agree that the Holy Spirit is operative in *every* believer and in the varied ministries of the church. Still every believer must answer the question of Acts 19:2. 'Have you received the Holy Spirit since you believed?'" ("Holy Spirit Gifts and Power," *New Spirit-Filled Life® Bible*).

1. Look up the following New Testament passages and then summarize what each says about "yielding the complete person into the guidance and indwelling of the Holy Spirit."

Romans 6:11–14

Romans 12:1, 2

Ephesians 4:17–24

2 Peter 1:3–11

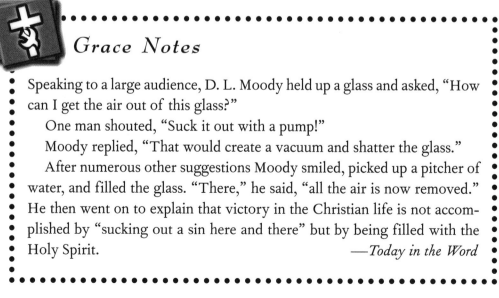

Grace Notes

Speaking to a large audience, D. L. Moody held up a glass and asked, "How can I get the air out of this glass?"

One man shouted, "Suck it out with a pump!"

Moody replied, "That would create a vacuum and shatter the glass."

After numerous other suggestions Moody smiled, picked up a pitcher of water, and filled the glass. "There," he said, "all the air is now removed." He then went on to explain that victory in the Christian life is not accomplished by "sucking out a sin here and there" but by being filled with the Holy Spirit.

—*Today in the Word*

The apostle Paul penned one of the great passages on living in the fullness of the Holy Spirit in Galatians 5:16–26. Read this passage and answer the following questions.

2.   What do you think Paul meant by the expressions *walk in the Spirit* (Gal. 5:16), *led by the Spirit* (5:18), and *live in the Spirit* (5:25)?

3.   Paul described the conflict between the flesh and the Holy Spirit as a battle of "lusts" (Gal. 5:17). What do you think is the burning desire of the flesh against the Spirit? What is the burning desire of the Holy Spirit against the flesh?

4.   How do *the works of the flesh* (Gal. 5:19–21) and *the fruit of the Spirit* (5:22–24) relate to the burning desires of these spiritual opponents?

5.   How might one become conceited and divisive while striving to *live in the Spirit* (Gal. 5:25, 26)?

Grace Notes

As I shut the door of the office after me, it seemed as if I met the Lord Jesus Christ face to face. It seemed to me that I saw Him as I would see any other man. He said nothing, but looked at me in such a manner as to break me right down at His feet. I fell down at His feet, wept aloud like a child, and made such confessions as I could with my choked utterance. It seemed to me that I bathed His feet in tears. I must have continued in this state for a good while. I returned to the front office, but as I turned and was about to take a seat by the fire, I received a mighty baptism of the Holy Ghost. Without any recollection that I had ever heard the subject mentioned by any person in the world, the Holy Spirit descended upon me in a manner that seemed to come in waves of liquid love; it seemed like the very breath of God. I wept aloud with joy and love.

—Charles Finney

6. If you have had a spiritual crisis experience since conversion that has led you into deeply committed discipleship to Jesus—whether or not you spoke in tongues at the time—describe it. How has this experience cemented your walk in the Spirit?

7. Circle the letter of the following statement that best describes your relationship with the Lord.

    a. I am a seeker trying to discover how to relate to God.

    b. I have received Jesus as my Savior, but I have not developed much spiritually since then.

    c. I am a growing disciple of Jesus Christ, but I have never encountered the Holy Spirit in a special way.

    d. I have had an experience with the Holy Spirit subsequent to conversion that has qualitatively changed my walk with Christ.

    e. I meet frequently with the Holy Spirit in encounters that renew and deepen my walk with Christ.

    f. Other:

8. The Spirit of God does not reproduce the image of Christ the same way in any two of God's children. He does not repeat Himself nor allow us to cram Him into the box of our expectations. Without trying to copy someone else and without envying anyone else, how would you like to see your walk in the Spirit develop and deepen in the near future?

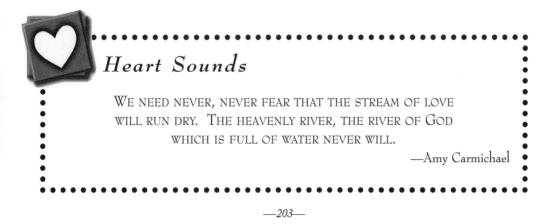

Heart Sounds

WE NEED NEVER, NEVER FEAR THAT THE STREAM OF LOVE WILL RUN DRY. THE HEAVENLY RIVER, THE RIVER OF GOD WHICH IS FULL OF WATER NEVER WILL.

—Amy Carmichael

SPEAKING WITH TONGUES

NOT ALL SPIRIT-FILLED Christians experience speaking in tongues, but many do. Probably no other spiritual phenomenon earmarks charismatic circles as readily as our openness to tongues as an evidence of the movement of the Holy Spirit in our midst. Paul Walker writes, "Speaking with tongues is a properly expected sign, affirming the Holy Spirit's abiding presence and assuring the believer of an invigorated living witness. It is not viewed as a *qualification for* fullness of the Holy Spirit, but as one *indication of* that fullness" ("Holy Spirit Gifts and Power," *New Spirit-Filled Life® Bible*).

1. Circle the letter of the following statement that best describes your experience with speaking in tongues.

    a. I haven't spoken in tongues, and my church is negative toward tongues.

    b. I haven't spoken in tongues yet, but my church is positive toward tongues.

    c. I have spoken in tongues privately even though my church is negative toward them.

    d. I speak in tongues privately as a devotional activity.

    e. I speak in tongues privately and during the services of my church.

    f. Other:

2. Summarize the teaching you have received and the personal attitudes you have toward the practice of speaking in tongues.

The next few questions will help you look at the biblical material reporting on or teaching speaking in tongues. Try to look at these passages as though you had never seen them before. Most of us have heard these Scriptures taught to prove a point rather than simply to explain them.

3. The Book of Acts reports incidents of speaking with tongues. Read these passages and summarize what each says regarding the purpose and significance of tongues.

Acts 2:1–18

Acts 10:44–48; 11:12–18

Acts 19:1–7

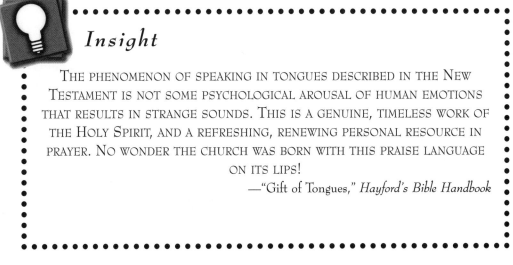

Insight

THE PHENOMENON OF SPEAKING IN TONGUES DESCRIBED IN THE NEW TESTAMENT IS NOT SOME PSYCHOLOGICAL AROUSAL OF HUMAN EMOTIONS THAT RESULTS IN STRANGE SOUNDS. THIS IS A GENUINE, TIMELESS WORK OF THE HOLY SPIRIT, AND A REFRESHING, RENEWING PERSONAL RESOURCE IN PRAYER. NO WONDER THE CHURCH WAS BORN WITH THIS PRAISE LANGUAGE ON ITS LIPS!

—"Gift of Tongues," *Hayford's Bible Handbook*

4. The first letter of Paul to the Corinthian church contains teaching on the spiritual gifts of speaking in tongues and interpreting tongues. Read the following passages from 1 Corinthians and summarize what each says regarding the purpose and significance of tongues.

1 Corinthians 12:7, 10, 11

1 Corinthians 12:29—13:1

1 Corinthians 14:2, 4, 14–19

1 Corinthians 14:6–13

1 Corinthians 14:21, 22

1 Corinthians 14:26–33

5. Looking back over the Corinthian passages, what would you say is the value of speaking in tongues privately and publicly?

Private tongues

Public tongues

Heart Sounds

Prayer and praise which speaks or sings in tongues may properly be described as using "spiritual language." . . . Of course, using the word "spiritual" for this prayer language isn't to suggest that spoken prayer or praise in one's native language is unspiritual or semi-spiritual. Each form of prayer is at a different dimension, and neither should be described as unworthy.

—"Spiritual Language," *Hayford's Bible Handbook*

6. If you have spoken in tongues, in the space below write a prayer telling God what this ministry of the Holy Spirit has meant to you. If you have not spoken in tongues, write a prayer expressing to God your openness to the fullness of the Holy Spirit as He desires it for you.

SIGNS AND WONDERS

WHILE TONGUES ARE a familiar manifestation of the Holy Spirit in charismatic circles and an occasional expression of the Spirit in many non-charismatic settings, miraculous activities in the form of "signs and wonders" are by definition extraordinary occurrences. Working miracles is listed in 1 Corinthians 12:10, 28 among the spiritual gifts the Holy Spirit might give to any Christian believer. Even believers who do not have the gift of working miracles may find themselves witnesses to or agents of the Spirit in the performance of a miraculous sign or wonder.

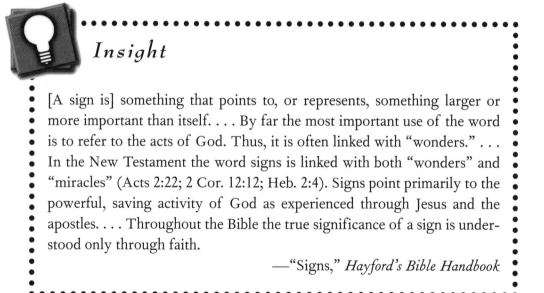

Insight

[A sign is] something that points to, or represents, something larger or more important than itself. . . . By far the most important use of the word is to refer to the acts of God. Thus, it is often linked with "wonders." . . . In the New Testament the word signs is linked with both "wonders" and "miracles" (Acts 2:22; 2 Cor. 12:12; Heb. 2:4). Signs point primarily to the powerful, saving activity of God as experienced through Jesus and the apostles. . . . Throughout the Bible the true significance of a sign is understood only through faith.

—"Signs," *Hayford's Bible Handbook*

1. Circle the letter of the following statement that best reflects your attitude toward reports of miraculous signs and wonders in churches, on the mission field, or here at home.

   a. Miracles happened in biblical times, but not today.

b. I'm skeptical, figuring people have been tricked or they have their own beliefs.

c. I figure miracles happen in cultures where belief in the supernatural is common but not in rationalistic cultures.

d. I want to believe God does miracles here and now, but I find myself looking for natural explanations for everything.

e. I believe miraculous signs and wonders occur when God engages the forces of Satan in power encounters.

f. I believe signs and wonders occur frequently and many people misinterpret or ignore them.

g. I have the gift of working miracles and use it.

h. Other:

2. What is the most compelling evidence of a miraculous event you have witnessed? What conclusions have you drawn from it (and other signs and wonders, perhaps) about God's use of miracles?

3. The spiritual gift of working miracles involves the person who has it with "(a) supernatural power to intervene and counteract earthly and evil forces, (b) a display of power giving the ability to go beyond the natural, and (c) cooperation with the gifts of faith and healing to bring authority over sin, Satan, sickness and the binding forces of this age" (Paul Walker, "Holy Spirit Gifts and Power," *New Spirit-Filled Life*® *Bible*). Other Christians may witness miraculous activity by God in response to prayer and faith quite apart

from the spiritual gift of miracles. Read the following biblical passages on signs and wonders and indicate whether you think the spiritual gift of working miracles, or a combination of prayer and faith is involved.

Acts 12:5–16

Acts 16:16–18

Acts 16:25, 26

2 Corinthians 10:3–6

James 5:14–18

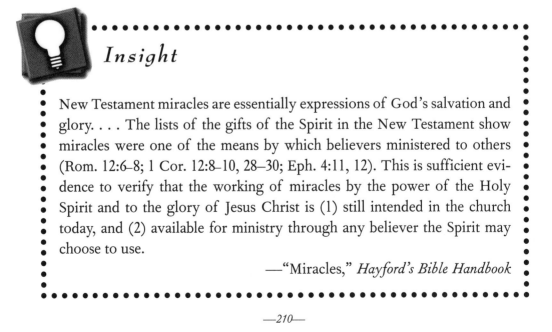

Insight

New Testament miracles are essentially expressions of God's salvation and glory. . . . The lists of the gifts of the Spirit in the New Testament show miracles were one of the means by which believers ministered to others (Rom. 12:6–8; 1 Cor. 12:8–10, 28–30; Eph. 4:11, 12). This is sufficient evidence to verify that the working of miracles by the power of the Holy Spirit and to the glory of Jesus Christ is (1) still intended in the church today, and (2) available for ministry through any believer the Spirit may choose to use.

—"Miracles," *Hayford's Bible Handbook*

4. Miraculous signs and wonders are not supernatural displays meant to amuse and astonish the saints of God. Signs and wonders are power displays to defeat and dismay the forces of evil, to establish new believers in their infant faith, or to give heart to discouraged believers. Once again read Acts 12:5–16. Imagine how this miracle functioned as a sign and wonder for each of the following groups.

The human and spiritual forces of evil

New believers in the Jerusalem church

Discouraged believers in the church

5. When you were a new believer in Jesus, how did the Lord show His strength to build your faith in Him?

6. How has the Lord shown His power in signs and wonders to encourage you when your faith has been weak?

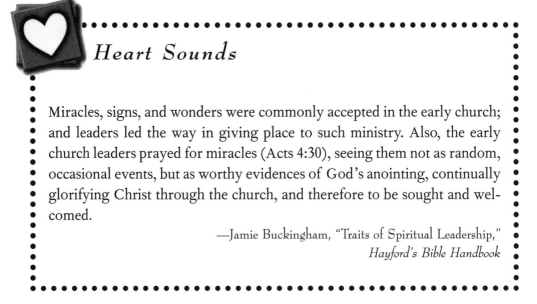

Heart Sounds

Miracles, signs, and wonders were commonly accepted in the early church; and leaders led the way in giving place to such ministry. Also, the early church leaders prayed for miracles (Acts 4:30), seeing them not as random, occasional events, but as worthy evidences of God's anointing, continually glorifying Christ through the church, and therefore to be sought and welcomed.

—Jamie Buckingham, "Traits of Spiritual Leadership,"
Hayford's Bible Handbook

7. Make a prayer list of situations or needs of people for which you can pray for God to intervene miraculously to defeat evil or strengthen His people. Use the following categories as a guide in your prayer. Before you begin, ask the Spirit of God to guide you in discerning and selecting situations that touch the heart of God.

Spiritual strongholds to be pulled down

Demonization

Physical healing

Impossible situations

Missions and evangelization

Other:

Refer to this list often in the days ahead. Pray regularly and fervently for these people and situations that may call for miraculous divine intervention. Ask others to join you in praying for some or all of these concerns. If you know someone who is a gifted intercessor, invite that person to join you in lifting these needs to the throne of God.

DIVINE HEALING

JESUS CONDUCTED AN extensive healing ministry and pointed to it as evidence that He was the Messiah (Luke 4:16–27; see Matt. 8:16, 17). Jesus sent His disciples in pairs to preach and heal (Matt. 9:1, 2). The apostles continued a healing ministry along with their preaching in the Book of Acts (5:14–16; 8:6, 7; 19:11, 12). James highlighted prayers for healing as a primary responsibility of the elders of the church (James 5:14–18). As with miracles in the preceding study, the Holy Spirit equips some believers with spiritual gifts of healing (1 Cor. 12:9, 30). They engage in healing in a unique way, but all believers are expected to pray for and believe in God for healing of themselves and others.

1. If you suspected you were seriously ill, which of the following actions would you probably take? Circle the letters of the statements that apply. Then in the blanks provided, number the actions you would take in the order in which you would probably take them.

____ a. Pray for God's guidance.

____ b. See a doctor for diagnosis.

____ c. Call for the elders of the church to anoint me with oil and pray for healing.

____ d. Pursue treatment with medicines, surgery, or other medical procedures.

____ e. Stay awake at night worrying.

____ f. Attend a healing service at my church.

____ g. Go to a healing service conducted by a nationally known healer.

____ h. Other:

2. What conclusions can you draw about your attitudes toward divine healing from your responses to item 1?

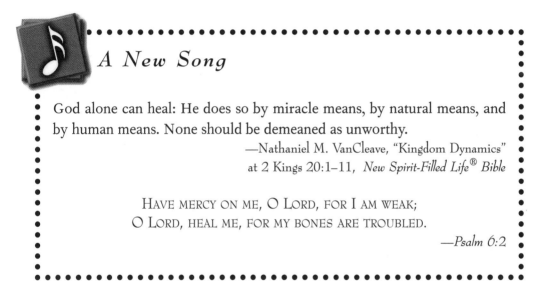

A New Song

God alone can heal: He does so by miracle means, by natural means, and by human means. None should be demeaned as unworthy.

—Nathaniel M. VanCleave, "Kingdom Dynamics"
at 2 Kings 20:1–11, *New Spirit-Filled Life® Bible*

HAVE MERCY ON ME, O LORD, FOR I AM WEAK;
O LORD, HEAL ME, FOR MY BONES ARE TROUBLED.

—*Psalm 6:2*

3. One of the most important biblical passages that establishes a theological basis for divine healing is the messianic prophecy about the rejection, suffering, and atoning death of Jesus found in Isaiah 53. Prayerfully and thoughtfully read Isaiah 53:1–5 and answer the following questions.

How does the New Testament interpret Isaiah 53:4 in Matthew 8:17?

According to Isaiah 53:4, 5, what various aspects of human misery did Jesus suffer and die to relieve?

When Isaiah said, *By His stripes we are healed*, how many kinds of healing did the prophet have in mind?

What do you think Jesus' attitude was toward sickness? Why do you think He connected its existence to sin in His atoning work?

What do you suppose the attitude of God is toward any illness you contract or injury you suffer? Why do you say that?

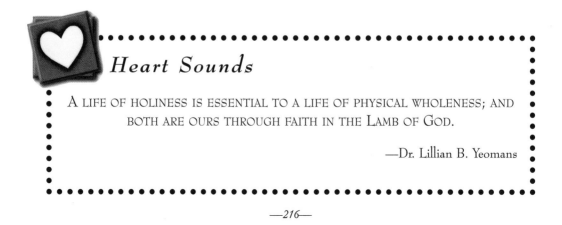

Heart Sounds

A LIFE OF HOLINESS IS ESSENTIAL TO A LIFE OF PHYSICAL WHOLENESS; AND BOTH ARE OURS THROUGH FAITH IN THE LAMB OF GOD.

—Dr. Lillian B. Yeomans

4. In 1 Corinthians 12:9, 30 the apostle Paul referred to gifts of healing. "Gifts of healing (a) refer to supernatural healing without human aid, and (b) may include divinely assisted application of human instrumentation and medical means of treatment" (Paul Walker, "Holy Spirit Gifts and Power," *New Spirit-Filled Life® Bible*). What characteristics or behaviors do you think would distinguish the healing ministry of someone with the gift of healing from the ministry of prayer and faith we all are expected to engage in on behalf of the sick?

5. Indicate which of the following biblical incidents you think illustrate the exercise of the spiritual gift of healing, and which illustrate ordinary believers employing prayer and faith to combat illness.

Acts 3:1–8

Acts 20:7–12

2 Corinthians 12:7–10

Philippians 2:25–30

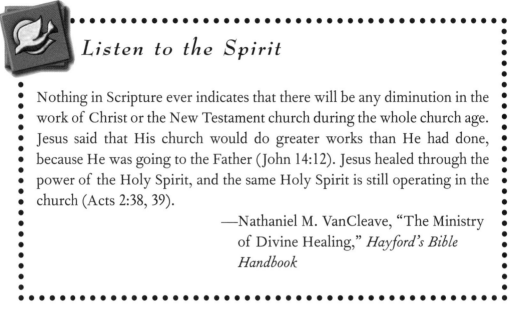

Listen to the Spirit

Nothing in Scripture ever indicates that there will be any diminution in the work of Christ or the New Testament church during the whole church age. Jesus said that His church would do greater works than He had done, because He was going to the Father (John 14:12). Jesus healed through the power of the Holy Spirit, and the same Holy Spirit is still operating in the church (Acts 2:38, 39).

—Nathaniel M. VanCleave, "The Ministry of Divine Healing," *Hayford's Bible Handbook*

6. List the people close to you who are ill and in need of God's healing touch. After each name, write down what you can do for them and what you might suggest they do to seek God's aid.

Insight

The differences between faith healing and divine healing are vast. . . . Faith healing finds its energy in self-generated, personal dynamism which claims to tap hidden resources within the individual or released through the "healer." But divine healing is ministered by the power of the Holy Spirit through divinely ordained promises, provision, and providence.

—"Healing," *Hayford's Bible Handbook*

8.   In the space provided, write a prayer of thanks to God for providing for deliverance from physical suffering as well as spiritual suffering through the death of Jesus. Spend some time meditating on the ramifications of this truth for you and for all of humanity.

FURTHER UP AND FURTHER IN

WHAT KIND OF journey have you started in the past eight weeks?

G. K. Chesterton, in the introduction to *The Everlasting Man*, imagined a boy setting off on a quest to find the rumored effigy and grave of a great giant. He was bored with rural life and wanted to do something exciting just once in his life. As he hiked up out of the valley where his father's farm lay, he glanced back at the world of his youth from a greater distance than ever before. He saw that "his own farm and kitchen-garden, shining flat on the hillside like the colours and quarterings of a shield, were but parts of some such gigantic figure, on which he had always lived, but which was too large and too close to be seen."

For eight weeks you have been looking at the pieces of the Spirit-filled life. Now it is time to step back and look at the big picture. What does God want to do in you as a result of your exposure to His Word and Spirit? Use this final time of meditation and prayer to review the past eight weeks and see what the whole "giant" looks like that you have examined one piece at a time.

Look through your workbook one chapter at a time. Reflect on your answers to the various exercises. Identify the primary lessons for you in each chapter in terms of content, attitude, and behavior.

1. Spirit-Filled Holiness

____The main thing I learned from the Bible.

____The primary attitude adjustment I need to make.

____The action the Holy Spirit will enable me to take.

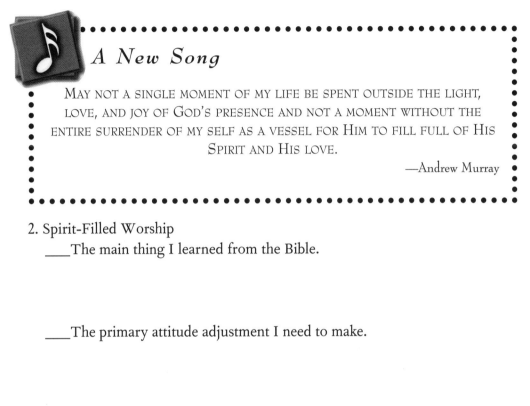

A New Song

MAY NOT A SINGLE MOMENT OF MY LIFE BE SPENT OUTSIDE THE LIGHT, LOVE, AND JOY OF GOD'S PRESENCE AND NOT A MOMENT WITHOUT THE ENTIRE SURRENDER OF MY SELF AS A VESSEL FOR HIM TO FILL FULL OF HIS SPIRIT AND HIS LOVE.

—Andrew Murray

2. Spirit-Filled Worship

____The main thing I learned from the Bible.

____The primary attitude adjustment I need to make.

____The action the Holy Spirit will enable me to take.

3. Spirit-Filled Kingdom Living

____The main thing I learned from the Bible.

____The primary attitude adjustment I need to make.

____The action the Holy Spirit will enable me to take.

4. Spirit-Filled Wisdom
   ____The main thing I learned from the Bible.

____The primary attitude adjustment I need to make.

____The action the Holy Spirit will enable me to take.

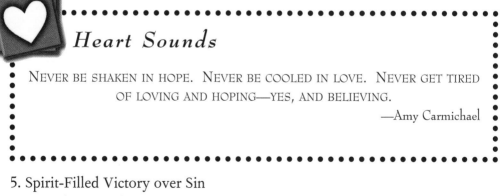

Heart Sounds

NEVER BE SHAKEN IN HOPE. NEVER BE COOLED IN LOVE. NEVER GET TIRED
OF LOVING AND HOPING—YES, AND BELIEVING.
—Amy Carmichael

5. Spirit-Filled Victory over Sin
   ____The main thing I learned from the Bible.

____The primary attitude adjustment I need to make.

____The action the Holy Spirit will enable me to take.

6. Spirit-Filled Relationships
    ____The main thing I learned from the Bible.

    ____The primary attitude adjustment I need to make.

    ____The action the Holy Spirit will enable me to take.

7. Spirit-Filled Leadership
    ____The main thing I learned from the Bible.

    ____The primary attitude adjustment I need to make.

    ____The action the Holy Spirit will enable me to take.

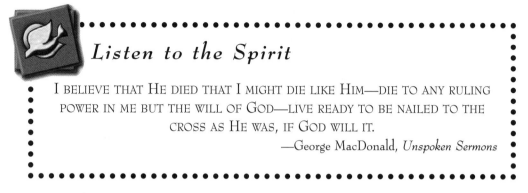

Listen to the Spirit

I BELIEVE THAT HE DIED THAT I MIGHT DIE LIKE HIM—DIE TO ANY RULING POWER IN ME BUT THE WILL OF GOD—LIVE READY TO BE NAILED TO THE CROSS AS HE WAS, IF GOD WILL IT.

—George MacDonald, *Unspoken Sermons*

8. Growth in the Spirit

____The main thing I learned from the Bible.

____The primary attitude adjustment I need to make.

____The action the Holy Spirit will enable me to take.

A New Song

MAY THE GRACE OF THE LORD JESUS CHRIST,
AND THE LOVE OF GOD,
AND THE FELLOWSHIP OF THE HOLY SPIRIT
BE WITH YOU ALL.

—*2 Corinthians 13:14*